The Debt Squads

The Debt Squads

The US, the Banks and Latin America

Sue Branford
Bernardo Kucinski

Zed Books Ltd
London New Jersey

The Debt Squads was first published in English by Zed Books Ltd, 57 Caledonian Road, London N1 9BU, UK and 171 First Avenue, Atlantic Highlands, New Jersey 07716, USA, in 1988. An earlier version, *A Ditadura da Dívida*, was first published in Portuguese by Editora Brasiliense, São Paulo, in 1987.

Cover designed by Andrew Corbett.
Typeset by Grassroots Typeset, London.
Figures drawn by Henry Iles, Mediumwave, London.
Printed and bound in the United Kingdom
at Bookcraft (Bath) Ltd, Midsomer Norton.

Second impression, 1990.

British Library Cataloguing in Publication Data

Branford, Sue, *1944–*
    The debt squads: the US, the banks and Latin America
    I. Developing countries. Governments. External debts
    I. Title II. Kucinski, Bernardo III. A ditadura da dívida.
    ·*English*
    336.3′433′1724

    ISBN 0-86232-790-3
    ISBN 0-86232-791-1 Pbk

Library of Congress Cataloging-in-Publication Data

Branford, Sue.
    [Ditadura da dívida. English]
    The debt squads: the US, the banks, and Latin America/
    Sue Branford, Bernardo Kucinski.
        p.   cm.
    Translation of: A ditadura da dívida.
    Includes index.
    ISBN 0-86232-790-3.   ISBN 0-86232-791-1   (pbk).
    1. Debts, External—Latin America. 2. Loans, Foreign—
    Latin America. 3. International Monetary Fund—Latin
    America. 4. Latin America—Economic conditions—1945-.
    5. United States—Foreign economic relations—Latin America.
    6. Latin America—Foreign economic relations—United States.
    I. Kucinski, Bernardo. II Title.
    HJ8514.5.B7313 1988
    336.3′435′098—dc 19   88-17215
                        CIP

Contents

Tables

Figures

Boxes

Glossary

amortisation repayment of principal of a loan over a period of years (as opposed to interest payment)

certificate of deposit (CD) a certificate, issued by a bank, in return for a deposit of money

capital flight transfer of money abroad, usually in dollars; often illegal, or irregular, in Latin America

central bank a bankers' bank and lender of last resort; the government's instrument for implementing its policies regarding the credit system

commercial banks privately owned banks, operating cheque current accounts, receiving deposits, taking and paying out money and making loans

commission handling charge, added to interest and spread to determine payment due on loan

crawling-peg devaluation scheme by which a local currency is devalued, usually against the US dollar, by a series of small, often weekly, devaluations

debt-bond swap the exchange, at a discount, of developing country foreign debt for bonds issued by the government of the developing country

debt-equity swap the exchange, at a discount, of developing country foreign debt for equity (i.e. shares) in local companies

debt service annual debt payments, consisting of both repayment of principal and payment of interest

debt-service ratio the ratio of debt-service payments (interest and principal) to the nation's export earnings

default non-payment of debt service

eurodollars dollars held by individuals and institutions outside the United States

euromarket the market for eurodollars and other currencies negotiated outside the country that issued them

floating interest rates interest rates, adjusted at regular intervals, usually every six months, to fix them at the rate at which the bank is currently borrowing money on the market

gold standard a system by which a country's central bank is obliged to give gold, at a fixed rate of exchange, in return for its currency

Libor London Inter-Bank Offered Rate. The rate of interest at which loans are offered to first-class banks on the London market

long- or medium-term debt debt repayable over a period longer than one year

money-centre banks a non-technical expression for the 11 largest US banks with the most extensive international financial operations

multi-year rescheduling a rescheduling of capital repayments for debt due over several years

moratorium cessation of debt-service payments

non-performing loans loans on which neither interest payment nor principal repayment is being made

prime rate the rate of interest charged in the US by commercial banks to first-class borrowers for short-term loans

provisions money put aside by banks against default on loans

reschedule to revise or postpone, usually for one year, dates on which capital repayments are supposed to be made. Interest payments are rarely rescheduled

secondary market a market for the resale of foreign debt, at a discount, outside the official market

shareholders' equity (or net worth) the capital actually owned by a bank (as distinct from its assets), that could be used to pay creditors should loans be defaulted

short-term debt debt repayable within one year

spread sum charged by banks over and above the interest rate and the commission; that part of debt payments earmarked to be banks' profit

syndicated loan loan made by a consortium of banks to a single borrower

terms of trade the ratio of the prices paid to a country for the goods it exports, compared with the prices it has to pay for its imports

Note to the reader

The United Nations Economic Commission for Latin America and the Caribbean (ECLAC) began life as the Economic Commission for Latin America (ECLA). The Spanish and Portuguese acronym for the same organisation is CEPAL. We have used ECLA when discussing specifically the Commission's early years, and CEPAL in some references to publications in the notes; otherwise ECLAC is used.

All references to dollars ($) are to US dollars.

One billion is taken to mean one thousand million.

Introduction

'I'll be judge, I'll be jury,' said cunning old Fury: 'I'll try the whole cause, and condemn you to death.'
Lewis Carroll, *Alice's Adventures in Wonderland*

General Secretary Gorbachev asks God whether there will ever be capitalism in the Soviet Union and is told: 'yes, but not in your lifetime.' President Reagan asks him whether there will ever be communism in the United States and gets the same answer. Then President Sarney asks whether Brazil will ever pay off its debts and the answer is: 'Yes, but not in My lifetime.'

Financial Times, 2 March 1988

An earlier version of this book was published in Portuguese in Brazil early in 1987. The publication came shortly before the Brazilian government took the highly controversial step of declaring a moratorium on interest payments on the foreign debt owed to private foreign banks. At the time, the foreign debt was — and, indeed, still is — very much a live issue, about which Brazilians felt passionately, and our book fed directly into this debate. The first edition sold out quickly, and was followed by a second.

We believe that our book is selling well among Brazilians because it looks at the crisis from the point of view of ordinary Latin Americans, who reaped few, if any, benefits from the huge borrowing, but are today being forced to pay for it, through either their labour or their poverty. We managed, to some extent at least, to break the monopoly that the 'makers' of the debt — that is, the ruling elites in Latin America and the bankers in the industrialised countries — have exercised, not only over the management of the debt crisis, but also over the very debate about the issue.

In Europe and the United States, this monopoly is still largely intact. Despite the efforts of some, notably, in Britain, War on Want's campaign and the work done by the World Development Movement, most ordinary people in the industrialised world see the Latin American debt crisis as a distant and complex technical issue which they do not understand and about which they have no strong feelings. The underlying outrage — that it is the governments and banks in the industrialised countries, through the International Monetary Fund, that have forced the poor in Latin America to cut yet further their already low living standards to finance a net transfer of wealth *out* of the region ($180 billion between 1981 and 1987) — is simply not known by the general public.

The climate of opinion is changing slowly. Over the last six months, as the scale of the current crisis has become clearer with the worldwide crash in stock markets and the slide of the dollar on the world's exchange markets, many economists are reassessing their views. But, even now, Latin America's role in the crisis is being largely ignored. Few recognise that the very same crisis in the world economy that for the last six years has been causing so much suffering in Latin America, is now creating the present shake-up in the industrialised countries. It is not even widely known that it was the reaction of the US money-centre banks to the Brazilian moratorium in February 1987 that sparked off the chain of events that led to the stock market crash six months later.

Both of us have done a great deal of financial reporting from Latin America, writing for bankers and decision-makers in the industrialised world. We found that changing our perspective and looking at the crisis, not from the viewpoint of the elites in the industrialised countries, but from that of the poor in Latin America, produced some remarkable results, which surprised us more than we had expected. In the first and third chapters, in which we give a snapshot of contemporary Latin America and look at the human cost of the debt crisis, we find that the scale of the confiscated income and the fall in living standards and investment have been dramatic, far greater than is suggested by the bankers' figures, which are geared to measuring the capacity of each country to continue paying the service on its debt. In the second chapter, in which we look at the way the IMF has operated in Latin America in recent years, we find that the very concepts and methodology used by the Fund reflect almost entirely the interests of the governments and bankers in the industrialised countries, not those of the people in the developing world.

In our investigations into the origin of the debt in the second part of the book, our basic argument is that the Latin American debt crisis arose as part of a crisis in the US economy, a crisis comparable to the 1930s Depression, but far more muted in the industrialised countries, though not in the developing world. In Chapter 4, we set the scene for the drama itself. We show that the present decline, which led to the snowballing of Latin American debt, began in the 1960s. The ingredients were a fall in the rate of profit in the United States, and chronic unemployment and inflation in the industrialised countries. In Chapters 5 and 6 we describe in some detail the two leading characters in our play: the international bankers, with their chaotic euromarket, the result of American expansion; and the dictators of the debt, the generals who, trained by Washington and encouraged by the local elites, came to power across much of the continent.

In Chapter 7 we start to follow, step by step, the unfolding of the drama itself, tracing from the first oil shock in the early 1970s to the Iranian revolution in 1979 the mechanisms brought into play by the dominant force — US capital — to transfer, postpone or redistribute the cost of the crisis. In Chapter 8, we show how Latin American governments were trapped into borrowing huge sums of money, most of which was immediately handed back to the banks in debt service. Between 1976 and 1981, Latin America borrowed an enormous \$272.9 billion. But over 60 per cent of this, \$170.5 billion, was immediately paid back to the banks in debt repayments or interest. Another \$22.9 billion remained with the banks, as reserves, which were a kind of additional guarantee for the debt itself. And an estimated \$56.6 billion was quickly sent abroad again as capital flight. Only \$22.9 billion effectively entered the continent to be used (or not) in productive investment. We had known beforehand that the old question — how on earth did Latin America spend so much money? — begged many more important questions, but, even so, the tiny proportion of the total debt that was actually spent in Latin America amazed us.

In Chapter 9, we deal with a development that has been grossly underrated in explaining the debt crisis: the economic counter-revolution undertaken under Reagan by the successors to the monetarists, known as the supply-siders. It was they who responded to the deteriorating US balance of payments, not by devaluing the dollar once again, as one might have imagined, but by increasing interest rates to attract capital from all over the world into the United States. This was, in practice, the *coup de grâce* for Latin America, already indebted beyond any reasonable limit, for it imposed on the region a new and vicious mechanism for extracting income. This may not have been the original intention of the supply-siders, but, once the catastrophic impact of their policies on the developing world became clear, they did nothing to change them; they carried on for years with the same policy, despite repeated protests from the Latin Americans.

The crisis, we argue, arose in the United States, but up to now its main expression has been the devastation of Latin America. In the 1930s, countries in the periphery of the world economy were affected by the Depression, but the main victims were workers in the USA, Britain and other economies at the centre, many of whom lost their jobs and suffered severe deprivation. Since then, these affluent countries have set up social welfare schemes that have effectively changed the character of unemployment.

This time it has been Latin America, still without the protection of social welfare schemes, that has suffered most severely. As well as grappling with serious problems of recession and high unemployment, caused largely by the IMF's 'adjustment' programmes, the Latin American economies have also been forced to make very heavy payments to the creditor banks in the industrialised countries, helping to increase liquidity and in this way to make further funds available for bailing out the US economy. But, as its impact in the industrialised countries has been so muted, the whole drama has been widely ignored. It was only after the collapse of the New York stock market on 19 October 1987 that the media began to admit that American capitalism might be in crisis. But the stock market crash is only one chapter in a longer tale, which is still dominated by the Latin American debt crisis.

As yet, there have been few signs of serious rifts between the industrialised powers as a result of the crisis. After the Brazilian moratorium, which, together with other delays in debt-servicing payments, brought some banks close to bankruptcy, the Japanese government decided to create its own version of the Marshall Plan, increasing its outlay on subsidised loans to the indebted countries from $700 million to $30 billion in the space of three years. But Japan is channelling its money largely through the international financial institutions, including the IMF, and is making disbursement conditional on the indebted country strengthening its links with these institutions. This is, perhaps, the most notable case of the industrial countries speaking with one voice on essential issues, despite squabbling over minor questions. In this way, the current crisis contrasts markedly with the 1930s Depression, which led to war between the central countries. Today, the war is against the periphery and it is a financial war.

In Chapter 10 we trace the evolution of the crisis in Latin America itself — the first round of reschedulings, the Latin American reaction, the multi-year deals, the new provisions by the banks, and, most recently, the first debt—bond swap. Despite the return to civilian rule in much of the continent, the Latin American elites have been hesitant and timorous. Despite new and intense contradictions having arisen from the debt crisis, they have been unwilling to break the old alliance with the elites in the industrialised countries. This has meant yet greater sacrifices for the Latin American people. Expressed very simply, the debt has synthesised and deepened the system of domination, creating a double need for the super-exploitation of Latin American workers. They are exploited to maintain the comfortable living styles of the local elites, as normally occurs under a capitalist system, and they are exploited so that an additional, exceptional tribute can be sent to the elites in the industrialised countries.

There has been considerable talk recently about a permanent solution to the debt crisis, now that the banks have decided first to increase their provisions for bad debts and, perhaps, start writing off part of the debt through the exchange, at a discount, of part of the old loans for new bonds with much greater repayment guarantees. But, as ever, the solution is for the banks, not for the people of Latin America. Under the new arrangements, Latin America will continue to be stretched to near breaking point so that it can go on paying the financial tribute. We believe that many more episodes are left in the debt saga, and that Latin America may not yet have been through the worst.

For Latin America it is not just a case of putting an end to the current transfer of wealth out of the region. In the opening chapters of this book, we examine the devastating effects of indebtedness on levels of investment and show that since 1982 the continent has taken several steps backwards in its development. Unless it can renovate its industry in a decade of accelerated technological change, the continent is running the risk of irreversible decline. After studying meticulously the Treaty of Versailles, the only episode in modern history that, through the scale of the confiscation, can be compared to the debt crisis, Lord Keynes warned that Germany could be reduced to a state of 'Asiatic poverty'. Events did not turn out like this, but the consequences of the treaty were no less tragic.

By adopting a new viewpoint — that of the colonised debtor, not that of the colonising banker — we have attempted to be both rational in our analysis and passionate in our intent. We have tried to be clear-headed and honest in our probings into the origins of the debt crisis and the mechanisms used to maintain the supremacy of the dollar, writing as ordinary observers who have taken advantage of academic work, but have not felt imprisoned by strict academic procedures. At the same time, we have not given up our right — indeed, we see it as our obligation — to take a position, as indeed we do in the conclusion when we say that, given the right external conditions, Latin America should default on its debt. Unlike those who say that the Latin American people are under a moral obligation to honour the debt, we say that their only obligation is to stop paying it.

The focus of this book is Latin America, which we know and love. But the main characteristics of the debt syndrome are similar, at times startlingly similar, in the other debt-burdened nations of the developing world, particularly in the Caribbean, Africa and certain parts of Asia, such as the Philippines. Many of our observations — and even, more tentatively, our prescriptions — are applicable to many other developing nations.

This book was planned, discussed and researched by two authors. Chapters 1, 2, 3, 8, 10 and 11 were written essentially by Sue Branford, with a contribution from Bernardo to the section on Brazil in Chapter 8. Chapters 4, 5, 6, 7 and 9 were written essentially by Bernardo Kucinski. The present text has been extensively updated and revised from the original Brazilian version.

We should like to give particular thanks to Italo Tronca for his comments on the manuscript, to John Rettie for his contribution to our discussions about Mexico, to Robert Molteno and Ralph Smith for their invaluable assistance with the English edition and, last but not least, to Mary Durran for her imaginative suggestion for the title.

1. The 1980s: A Lost Decade

An examination of the real scale of the transfer of income from Latin America to the creditor banks

> We are caught up in the Third World War, an economic war. It is an undeclared war, over the extortionate interest rates of the debt. The corpses are already piling up, but the aggressors maintain that the war doesn't exist, that the dead are alive and healthy.
>
> **Fidel Castro**, in an interview published in *Juros Subversivos*, by the Brazilian journalist, Joelmir Beting, 1985

To service its foreign debt, Latin America sent to the banks in the industrialised countries, in net terms, $159.1 billion from the end of 1981 to the end of 1986. By the end of 1987, the total is estimated to have reached $180 billion. It is more than the total cost to the US treasury of the Vietnam war.[1] It has meant sending abroad each year about 4−5 per cent of the region's economic output and is the greatest transfer ever of money from a poor developing region to the industrialised world.

The transfer of resources out of the region has been far heavier than was the net influx of money into the region in the late 1970s, when Latin America was raising one enormous loan after another on the world financial market. As we show later, only about $23 billion actually entered the region between 1976 and 1981, the years of heaviest borrowing. This is about one-eighth of the amount that was sent out of Latin America between 1981 and 1987. In terms of the net transfer of resources, the debt has already been repaid several times over, even allowing for inflation and for the payment of what in the 1970s was considered a 'normal' rate of interest.

Despite this huge transfer of wealth out of the region, it has not been enough to pay all the interest on the debt, let alone cover Latin America's other external commitments, such as dividends and royalties on foreign investment, freight, and the repayment of loans from the international financial organisations. So, even though Latin America has rolled over almost all its commercial loans and attempted to pay only the interest, it has had to borrow even more money from the banks. The result, paradoxically, has been that Latin America's gross foreign debt grew by almost a half from the end of 1981 to the end of 1987, despite the huge tribute being paid to the banks (*see* Figure 1.1).

The people of Latin America have thus received the worst of both worlds (*see* Table 1.1). During the boom years of abundant petrodollars, an enormous foreign debt was incurred in their name, but relatively little was done to promote their development. And during the recent years of recession, they have been forced to accept enormous sacrifices, so that billions of dollars can be sent abroad in debt-servicing, but they have ended up with an even larger foreign debt, for which they will have to go on sacrificing their development, unless they can force through far-reaching changes in the rules of the game, far more radical than the concessions that have so far been extracted from the creditors.

Figure 1.1
Latin America: The Inexorable growth of the Foreign Debt.*

($ bn)

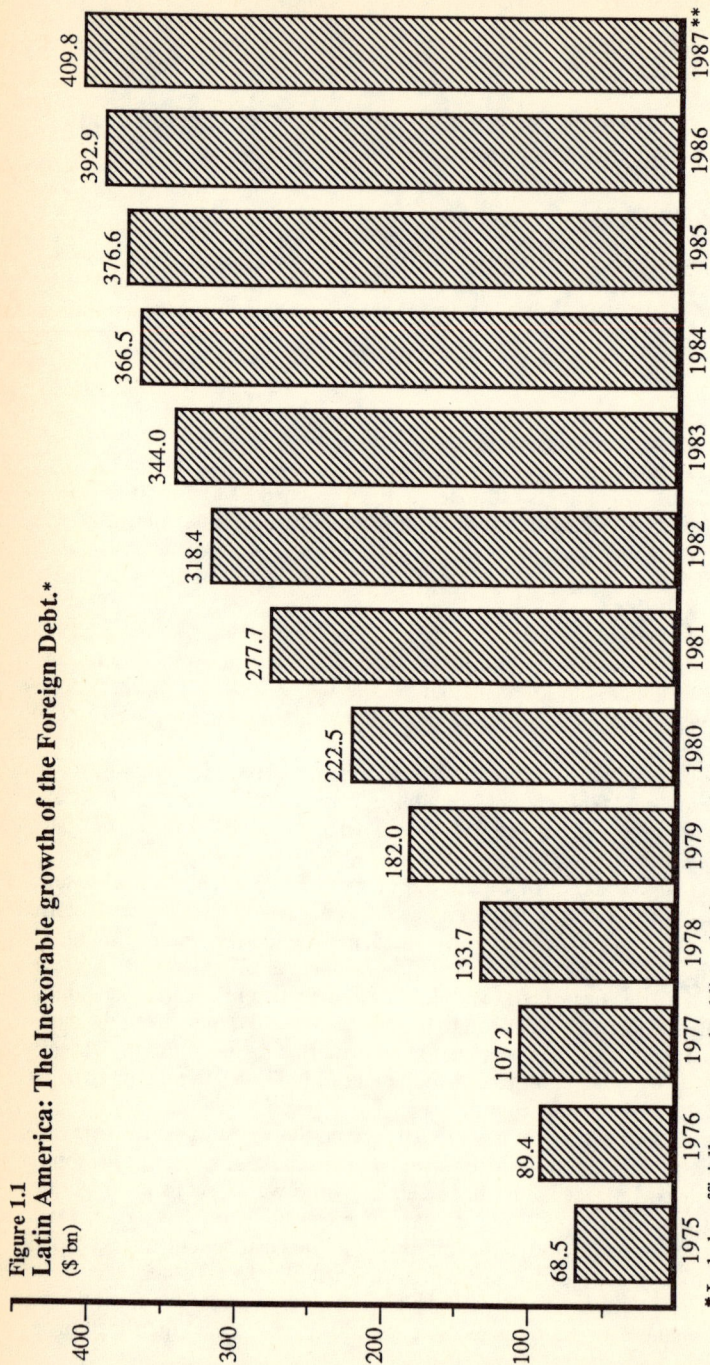

* Includes officially guaranteed public and private external debt, long- and short-term non-guaranteed debt with institutions reporting to the Bank for International Settlements.

**Preliminary figures

Source: ECLAC

A decade of de-development

The heavy transfer of resources out of the region has entailed superhuman efforts. Both living standards and investment (*see* Tables 1.4 and 1.5) have fallen heavily, while inflation (*see* Table 1.2) has soared. Development has not just come to a standstill; it has taken several steps backwards. Latin America has experienced 'de-development', comparable to Britain's de-industrialisation, except that the process has been faster and the social cost far greater. Though some Latin American countries, notably Brazil and Peru, have rebelled and have succeeded in reversing some of the trends (though only temporarily), Latin America as a whole is still experiencing very low, or negative, per capita growth, with investment running at an alarmingly low level.

Table 1.1
Latin America: the worst of both worlds

Latin America squeezes its economy hard . . .

Year-end change	1981	1982	1983	1984	1985	1985/80
Gross domestic investment (%)	−0.8	−13.9	−19.2	1.5	4.3	−26.9
GDP per capita (%)	−1.9	−3.7	−4.8	1.4	1.1	−8.9
Terms of trade (1970 = 100)	115	84	83	86	84	−30.6%
GDP per capita consumed in region* (%)	−1.3	−11.3	−5.3	−6.5	3.6	−19.7
Trade balance ($ bn)	−1.7	9.1	31.5	38.7	34.4	111.9

. . . but still needs to borrow more

	1981	1982	1983	1984	1985	1985/80
Net interest payments ($ bn)	26.7	35.0	31.4	34.8	33.1	161.0
Gross foreign debt ($ bn)	277.7	318.4	344.0	360.4	368.0	145.5

* The gross domestic product consumed or invested within the region has been calculated by subtracting from the gross domestic product net foreign remittances and the trade surplus. To calculate the variation in the volume of goods and services available in the region, the trade surplus each year has been standardised at 1980 terms of trade for this calculation alone.

Sources: ECLAC and IDB annual reports

The social cost has been particularly high because of the adverse world conditions in which the transfer of resources has occurred and because of the intransigent stance adopted by the creditors. In the wake of the Mexican crisis in mid-1982, lending to Latin America from the international banks came to a virtual halt. This meant that, far from making debt repayments, the Latin American countries could continue to pay the interest on their foreign debts only if they somehow or other generated the dollars from their own economies, a task that was almost impossible because of the huge amounts that had to be paid as a result of the extraordinarily high rates of interest on the world market at that time. But, despite this, the banks made it clear that they would reschedule the foreign debts of the Latin American countries only if they continued to pay as much of the interest as they possibly could. To ensure that the flow of interest payments continued, even if this required brutal changes in the local economy, the banks insisted that the Latin American governments call in the International Monetary Fund (IMF).

Table 1.2
Latin America: the inflationary spiral
(consumer prices, annual % change)

	1981	1982	1983	1984	1985	1986	1987*
Brazil	91.2	97.9	179.2	203.3	228.0	58.4	337.9
Mexico	28.7	98.8	80.8	59.2	63.7	105.7	143.6
Argentina	131.2	208.7	433.7	688.0	385.4	81.9	178.3
Venezuela	10.8	7.9	7.0	18.3	5.7	12.3	36.1
Chile	9.5	20.7	23.6	23.0	26.4	17.4	22.9
Peru	72.7	72.9	125.1	111.5	158.3	62.9	104.8
Colombia	27.5	24.1	16.5	18.3	22.3	21.0	24.7
Ecuador	17.9	24.3	52.5	25.1	24.4	27.3	30.6
Uruguay	29.4	20.5	51.5	66.1	83.0	76.4	59.9
Bolivia	25.2	296.5	328.2	2,177.2	8,170.5	66.0	10.5
Latin America	**57.6**	**84.8**	**131.1**	**185.2**	**275.3**	**64.6**	**187.1**

* Preliminary figures

Source: ECLAC

At first, the governments could use the reserves they had built up in the late 1970s, when the banks had fallen over themselves to lend. But this supply was exhausted in a surprisingly short period and Latin America had to find the money — far more painfully — from its trade surplus, which is its only important regular source of hard currency.

It is always gruelling for a developing region to run a heavy trade surplus, for it necessarily entails exporting more goods and services than are imported back into the region. In other words, it means sending abroad part of an economic product that is already pitifully small for the needs of the local inhabitants. But, in Latin America's case, the social cost of achieving the surplus was increased significantly by the world recession which harmed the region's trade prospects in two important ways.

First of all, world trade stagnated, leaving very little scope for Latin America to increase the volume of its exports. Secondly, it led to a big drop in the world price of primary products, which are almost always more vulnerable than manufactured goods to the impact of a world recession and are still the region's most important source of export earnings. The price of basic products — food crops, tropical beverages (such as coffee and cocoa), agricultural raw materials and metals — dropped from an index of 100 in 1980 to 72.3 in 1985.[2] It was the most important factor accounting for the 31 per cent decline in the region's terms of trade (that is, the unit price of its exports compared with that of its imports) during the same period (*see* Table 1.1).

So Latin America was doubly hurt: stagnant world trade meant that it could not boost its trade surplus by increasing exports, which would have been the least painful option, but only by slashing imports; and deteriorating terms of trade meant that the region had to keep on sending abroad a larger and larger volume of goods to earn the same number of dollars. As a result, the region had to reduce imports violently — more violently than ever before in its history — in order to free the dollars required for debt-servicing.

Latin American trade went from a small deficit of $1.7 billion in 1981 to an accumulated surplus of $113.6 billion over the next four years. It was the greatest turnaround in foreign trade ever achieved by a developing region. But the falling terms of trade meant that the effort required by the region to run this surplus was even greater than suggested by these figures.

From 1980 to 1985, as the result of a determined export drive, Latin America achieved a 23 per cent increase in the volume of the goods it exported. But falling prices of basic products meant that overall export earnings did not rise, but actually fell slightly, by just under 1 per cent. During the same period, Latin America slashed the volume of its imports by an enormous 60 per cent, but rising prices of manufactured goods meant that the decline in value was only 41 per cent (*see* Table 1.3).

Table 1.3
Latin America: the external squeeze
(imports, annual level of) ($ bn)

	1981	1982	1983	1984	1985	% change 1985/81	1986	1987*
Brazil	22.1	19.4	15.4	13.9	12.8	−42.1	14.0	15.1
Mexico	24.0	14.5	8.5	11.3	13.5	−43.7	11.4	12.0
Argentina	8.4	4.8	4.1	4.1	3.7	−56.0	4.3	4.9
Venezuela	12.1	11.0	13.2	7.9	6.6	−45.4	7.7	8.2
Chile	6.5	3.6	2.8	3.3	2.9	−55.4	3.1	4.0
Peru	3.8	3.8	2.7	2.1	1.8	−52.1	2.5	2.9
Colombia	4.8	5.4	4.5	4.0	4.0	−16.7	3.7	3.9
Ecuador	2.7	2.5	1.9	1.8	1.7	−58.8	1.6	2.1
Uruguay	1.6	1.0	0.7	0.7	0.7	−56.3	0.8	1.0
Bolivia	0.7	0.4	0.5	0.4	0.4	−36.8	0.6	0.7
Latin America	**97.6**	**78.3**	**56.0**	**58.8**	**57.6**	**−41.0**	**59.7**	**65.5**

* Preliminary figures

Sources: ECLAC and IDB

The recession unleashed by the about-turn in trade was appalling. Many local factories were forced to close, because of shortages of imported components. Millions were thrown out of work in a region without unemployment benefit. Inflation soared and the real value of wages dropped heavily. Domestic investment fell, as both national and transnational companies cancelled expansion plans while they waited for the storm to pass. The average investment ratio (that is, total investment as a percentage of GDP) for Latin America's seven largest economies dropped from 23 per cent in 1980/81 to 17 per cent in 1984 (*see* Table 1.5). Per capita gross domestic product declined by 8.9 per cent between 1980 and 1985 (*see* Table 1.4). If the impact of both falling terms of trade and the net transfer of resources out of the region are taken into account, then per capita income, consumed or invested within the region, fell by about one-fifth (19.7 per cent).

Table 1.4
Latin America in crisis, 1981-85

Gross Domestic Product
(% change)

	1981	1982	1983	1984	1985	1985/80	1986	1987*
Brazil	−2.0	1.4	−2.7	4.8	7.0	**8.4**	8.2	3.0
Mexico	8.3	0.0	−5.2	3.5	3.5	**9.8**	−4.0	1.0
Argentina	−6.7	−6.3	3.0	2.0	−3.0	**−10.9**	6.0	2.0
Venezuela	−1.0	−1.3	−5.6	−1.1	0.0	**−8.7**	5.5	1.5
Chile	5.2	−13.1	−0.5	6.2	2.0	**−1.7**	5.4	5.5
Peru	3.7	−0.2	−12.0	4.4	2.0	**−2.8**	8.0	7.0
Colombia	2.3	1.0	1.2	3.6	2.0	**10.7**	5.1	5.5
Ecuador	3.8	1.1	−1.2	4.8	4.9	**10.9**	3.0	−3.0
Uruguay	1.0	−10.7	−5.9	−1.2	0.0	**−16.2**	6.6	5.5
Bolivia	0.7	−6.6	−8.6	−3.7	−2.5	**−19.2**	−2.9	1.5
Latin America	**0.4**	**−1.5**	**−2.5**	**3.2**	**2.8**	**2.3**	**3.7**	**2.6**

Gross Domestic Product per capita
(% change)

	1981	1982	1983	1984	1985	1985/80	1986	1987*
Brazil	−4.2	−0.9	−4.9	2.5	4.8	**−3.0**	5.9	1.0
Mexico	5.4	−2.6	−7.6	0.9	0.7	**−3.6**	−6.3	−1.2
Argentina	−8.2	−7.8	1.4	0.4	−4.5	**−17.7**	4.4	0.7
Venezuela	−3.9	−4.1	−8.2	−3.8	−2.7	**−20.8**	2.6	−1.1
Chile	3.6	−14.4	−2.1	4.5	0.2	**−9.1**	3.7	3.6
Peru	1.0	−2.7	−14.3	1.8	−0.4	**−14.6**	5.3	4.5
Colombia	0.1	−1.1	−1.0	1.4	0.1	**−0.5**	3.7	3.1
Ecuador	0.8	−1.8	−4.4	1.7	−0.3	**−4.0**	0.2	−5.8
Uruguay	0.3	−11.3	−6.5	−1.9	−0.9	**−19.1**	5.9	4.9
Bolivia	−1.9	−9.1	−11.0	−6.3	−5.0	**−29.4**	−1.6	−1.0
Latin America	**−0.9**	**−3.7**	**−4.8**	**0.8**	**0.5**	**−8.9**	**1.4**	**0.5**

* Preliminary figures

Sources: ECLAC and IDB annual reports

Big debtors suffer less

Bankers, who have dominated the discussion of the debt crisis in the industrialised countries and have successfully depoliticised the issue, turning it into a technical question of 'financial flows', have concentrated heavily on the three biggest debtors, even referring among themselves to the 'MBA' problem. This is because these three — Mexico, Brazil and Argentina, accounting for 68 per cent of Latin America's total debt — are the countries that represent the main threat to the world banking system. But, from a Latin American point of view, such an assessment is simplistic and misleading. What is important for these countries is not the potential damage that could be inflicted on the creditor nations, but the actual harm they, the debtors, have suffered. And here, far from the big countries bearing the brunt of the damage, there are clear indications that the two biggest debtors — Brazil and Mexico — have been more successful than their neighbours in mitigating the impact of the crisis.

In our analysis, we have looked at the ten nations with the biggest foreign debts in absolute terms. In 1985, imports into all of these countries ran at a substantially lower level than in 1981 (*see* Table 1.3). In almost all cases, the reduction was at least 40 per cent, with no differences between the two big debtors and other countries. It was a desperate attempt by all the countries to free more resources for debt-servicing by cutting imports to the bone.

The differences emerge when you look at the impact on the domestic economy of this sudden contraction (*see* Table 1.4). In Brazil and Mexico, per capita output fell by 3 −4 per cent. This is serious enough for the people in these countries, particularly when you remember that neither Brazil nor Mexico has a comprehensive system of social welfare and that the fall in average income was greater than the fall in average output, because of the much larger volume of goods being exported, and thus not being consumed locally.

But these reductions pale into insignificance when compared with the ravages suffered by all the other countries (except Colombia, which constantly figures in the tables as much less affected than the other medium-sized countries). In four countries — Bolivia, Venezuela, Uruguay and Argentina — the decline was more than 17 per cent. The worst affected of all was Bolivia, where the fall was a mind-boggling 29 per cent.

There seem to be several interlinked reasons for the greater resilience of the two big debtors. First of all, their larger and more diversified economies are much less dependent on imports. Particularly in the case of Brazil, relatively few imports, apart from oil, are essential for the functioning of the economy, and imports represent a smaller percentage of economic output than in the rest of Latin America, except in Colombia. This means that the same percentage decline in imports has a lesser recessionary impact.

Secondly, the Brazilian and Mexican foreign debts, though the largest in absolute terms, are smaller with respect to the size of their economies than in all but one other Latin American country (*see* Figure 1.2). (The exception is again Colombia, which may help to explain its greater resilience to the debt crisis.) In Bolivia, the foreign debt is actually larger than the total economic output.

These two factors raise an important question about the so-called 'debt service ratio', so beloved of bankers and economists, which is supposed to measure a country's debt burden. This ratio takes debt service (that is, interest payments plus repayments of principal) and compares it with export earnings. The higher the ratio, the heavier the burden. It now becomes clear that, like the bankers' obsessive

Table 1.5
Latin America: the fall in investment

Gross domestic investment
($ bn)*

	1980	1984	1984/1980 change(%)	1986
Brazil	66.4	41.9	−36.9	46.3
Mexico	51.5	34.2	−33.6	35.3
Argentina	18.3	9.0	−53.0	8.7
Venezuela	14.8	10.0	−32.4	12.1
Chile	6.5	4.0	−38.5	4.2
Peru	4.0	3.3	−17.5	3.1
Colombia	6.5	7.1	9.2	6.2
Ecuador	3.0	2.0	−33.3	2.2
Uruguay	1.6	0.8	−50.0	0.6
Bolivia	1.0	0.7	−30.0	0.6
Latin America	**187.1**	**123.8**	**−33.8**	**125.7**

Total investment as % of GDP

	1980-81 (average)	1982	1983	1984
Argentina	21.0	19.0	16.2	14.7
Brazil	23.5	24.3	20.8	17.9
Chile	22.7	12.3	10.4	14.9
Colombia	20.0	20.9	19.8	19.4
Mexico	29.4	22.5	18.9	18.5
Peru	21.0	23.9	20.8	17.1
Venezuela	23.7	26.5	14.7	16.0
Average of 7 countries	**23.0**	**21.3**	**17.4**	**17.0**

* in constant 1986 dollars.

Sources: ECLAC, IDB

concern with the big debtors at the expense of the smaller ones, this ratio is biased. It does not measure, objectively, the social cost of debt servicing in the local economy (which, from the debtor's point of view, is the real burden) but, instead, assesses the intensity of the external squeeze required for debt-servicing. What it is really looking at is the probability of the debtor being in a position to go on paying the service in the future. It reflects the interests of the creditors, not of the debtors.

An index of the real debt burden

To give a clearer idea of the real debt burden, we have calculated the ratio of interest payments (which is practically the only kind of debt-service payment being made at present) with respect to economic output (*see* Table 1.6). As is to be

Figure 1.2
Latin American foreign debt: per capita and its share of GDP, 1985

Per capita foreign debt 1985 ($)

Foreign debt as % of GDP 1985

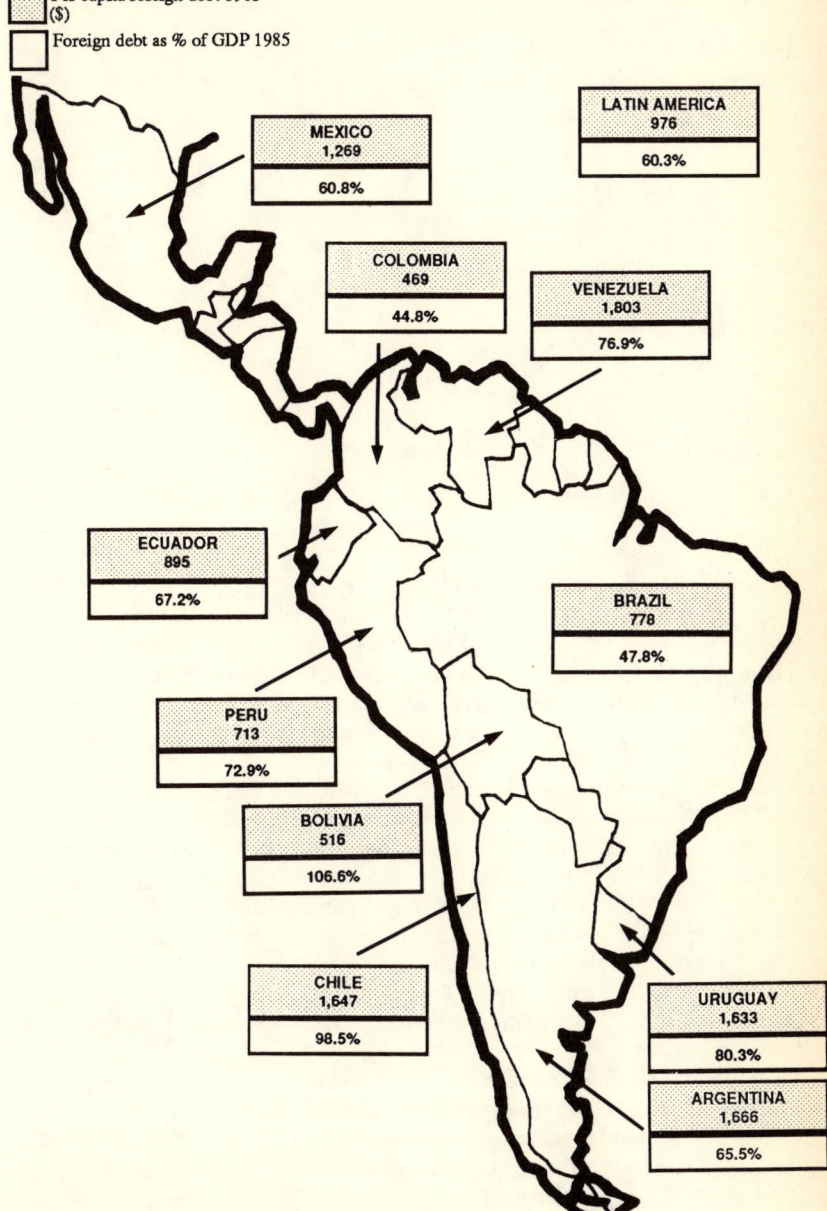

LATIN AMERICA
976
60.3%

MEXICO
1,269
60.8%

COLOMBIA
469
44.8%

VENEZUELA
1,803
76.9%

ECUADOR
895
67.2%

BRAZIL
778
47.8%

PERU
713
72.9%

BOLIVIA
516
106.6%

CHILE
1,647
98.5%

URUGUAY
1,633
80.3%

ARGENTINA
1,666
65.5%

Sources: ECLAC & IDB

expected, the burden is lighter in Brazil and Mexico than in all other countries (except Colombia). Bolivia, Venezuela, Chile and Ecuador appear as the countries struggling under the heaviest loads.

Table 1.6
The debt burden in Latin America
Interest payments as a percentage of gross domestic products

	1981	1982	1983	1984	1985	1986	1987*
Brazil	4.5	5.5	4.7	4.9	4.2	3.0	2.8
Mexico	4.5	6.0	5.7	6.6	5.2	4.9	4.6
Argentina	3.7	7.4	8.0	8.1	8.5	6.2	6.1
Venezuela	5.5	8.0	7.7	7.0	6.6	3.5	3.0
Chile	2.4	9.7	8.0	9.2	6.9	6.7	5.3
Peru	5.9	3.9	4.9	5.6	4.0	3.1	2.5
Colombia	3.9	2.9	2.7	3.4	4.2	3.9	4.0
Ecuador	7.3	7.3	7.2	7.7	7.7	6.1	6.6
Uruguay	8.4	4.3	4.6	5.2	5.8	3.5	3.1
Bolivia	2.5	10.8	10.9	15.4	11.3	9.0	7.3
Latin America	**4.3**	**5.7**	**5.3**	**5.7**	**4.8**	**3.6**	**3.4**

* estimate

Source: ECLAC, IDB

The figures are roughly in line with the other indicator that we have used — per capita economic output (*see* Table 1.4). Both sets of figures suggest that the crisis has been most severe in Bolivia: interest payments accounted on average for about 10 per cent of its output, and per capita production fell by 29 per cent between 1980 and 1985. Venezuela, Argentina, Uruguay, Peru and Chile all suffered heavily, in terms of both the burden of interest payments and the fall in per capita output. Brazil and Mexico fared better than all the other countries (except Colombia and, somewhat unexpectedly, Uruguay in the case of interest payments).

The crisis has meant that, for Latin America, the 1980s have already become a lost decade. Even if the region had resumed in 1987 its average post-war growth rate of 4−5 per cent, it would only have reached its 1980 per capita output by the early 1990s. If the crisis continues in an attenuated form for the rest of this decade, as seems likely, then the continent's living standards right up to the year 2000 will be compromised. Worse still, the failure to invest and to develop in the 1980s, a decade of crucial technological change, may be condemning much of Latin America, particularly the smaller countries, to permanent underdevelopment and dependence.

The present crisis is reminiscent in some ways of the Great Depression in the early 1930s. In the 1920s, Latin America borrowed heavily, largely because loans were easy to raise and interest rates were low. But in 1928 and 1929, interest rates rose in the US, because foreign capital was required to help finance what with hindsight can be seen as an artifical and precarious consumer boom, the last fling before the Great Crash. With the US attracting much of the available money, the flow of capital to Latin America fell to only a third of the level required for full debt servicing.

Just as today, Latin America tried for a while to make up the shortfall through increasing exports while reducing imports. But the 1929−32 crash put an end to this strategy. As world trade collapsed, prices for Latin America's main commodities tumbled. Though Latin American governments imposed import restrictions and foreign exchange controls, as well as devaluing their currencies, they could not avoid insolvency.

In 1930, Bolivia was the first country to stop servicing its debt, but, by the end of 1933, all but two — Haiti and Argentina — had followed suit. And they were both special cases, as one author explains:

> Haiti's good behaviour can be best explained by the presence of US Marines on its soil. In Argentina, politically powerful landowners prevailed; access to British markets for their grain and beef could not be lost at any cost. The British would allow Argentina to sell its goods freely to Great Britain only if debt payments were serviced punctually. Argentina kept up payments through the 1930s, but the sacrifices imposed on urban industrialists and workers played a major role in bringing the populist regime of Juan Perón to power in the 1940s.[3]

Though the battering suffered by the Latin American economies during the present period is comparable to the recession of the early 1930s, there are important differences. First of all, the crisis in the 1930s erupted in the centre and, defying efforts by the world powers to control it, spread to the periphery. The Latin American default was largely a by-product of the upheaval in the centre. Though today's crisis also arose in the centre, as we shall see in detail in later chapters of this book, its effects have, in contrast, only been felt dramatically in the periphery. Far from losing control, the international banks have retained the initiative and even made profits out of Latin America's vulnerability.

Secondly, the Latin American default in the 1930s did not lead to a world banking crisis. The banks had not lent on their own behalf — as they were to do in the 1970s — but had acted as intermediaries for thousands of small investors. As a result, though the Latin American default spelt disaster for many individuals, it did not threaten directly the stability of the world banking system. In contrast, a generalised default by Latin American debtors today could still lead to the insolvency of the leading commercial banks in the industrialised world, despite their recent efforts to increase their provisions against possible non-payment.

Thirdly, the role of the US on the world stage has changed. In the 1930s and 1940s, it was intent on replacing the British as the leading world power. As a result, it was far more conciliatory in the areas of the world where it was gaining control. This even implied a certain tolerance of default. Today, the US regards Latin America as part of its backyard, which does not need to be treated with kid gloves.

Fourthly — and most importantly of all — the 1929−32 Great Depression indirectly brought the region real benefits. For the sudden collapse in the external sector proved a real boost to local industry, which began to substitute imports. After a few difficult years, most nations made a rapid recovery. Indirectly, the

Great Depression pushed Latin America into the next important phase of economic development. No comparable benefit has yet emerged from the current crisis. On the contrary, Latin America has been experiencing 'de-development'. The only positive development has been the tentative and hesitant growth of political opposition to the IMF and all it represents. But, as we shall see, progress in developing a viable, alternative strategy has been agonizingly slow.

Notes

1. According to Barbara Tuchman, in *The March of Folly*, (Abacus, 1984) p. 471, the US spent $150 billion more than its normal military budget during the years of the Vietnam war.
2. *South*, June 1986.
3. Jeff Frieden, 'On Borrowed Time', in *Report on the Americas,* NACLA, March—April 1985.

2. The Bleeding of Latin America: the IMF at Work

A look at how the IMF forced the Latin American people to service the debt

As for Washington's insistence on fiscal purity, this was perhaps a trifle unseemly on the part of a nation which had financed so much of its own development by inflation, wild cat paper money and bonds sold to foreign investors and subsequently repudiated. If the criteria of the International Monetary Fund had governed the United States in the nineteenth century, our own economic development would have taken a great deal longer. In preaching fiscal orthodoxy to developing nations, we were somewhat in the position of the prostitute who, having retired on her earnings, believes that public virtue requires the closing down of the red-light district.

The US historian **Arthur Schlesinger**, in *A Thousand Days*, (André Deutsch, 1965) p. 158

The chief agent for ensuring that Latin America carries out the huge transfer of resources has been the International Monetary Fund (IMF). It was called in by the commercial banks, which told one Latin American country after another that they would reschedule its huge debts only if it accepted an IMF austerity programme. Though the intensity of the 'adjustment' demanded by the IMF has varied considerably, largely as a result of political considerations (*see* Chapter 4), the basic philosophy has remained the same and is worth examining in some detail.

The methodology of the IMF

The IMF takes as its starting point the country's balance of payments. This registers all transactions carried out abroad and is divided into two big sections, the current account and the capital account. In general terms, the current account measures transactions that are basically under the control of the government of the country in question: its trade balance, with its outlay on imports and its export earnings; and its expenditure on foreign services, such as freight and foreign tourism. In contrast, the capital account measures inflows and outflows of foreign capital, be it investment by foreign companies or loans from foreign banks.

A leading IMF official told the *Financial Times* how the procedure worked: 'First, you look at what the capital account can be over the next few years, then you derive the current account.'[1] In other words, the IMF begins its analysis by looking at capital flows, estimating how much the banks can be expected to lend and how much foreign companies can be expected to invest. It then looks at how much hard currency the country needs, to cover both the remittance of royalties and dividends, and debt-servicing payments, both interest and repayment of capital. On the basis of these estimates, the IMF then prepares an 'adjustment' programme to force the country either through an increase in exports or, more frequently, through a reduction in imports, to produce the necessary dollars. Under the IMF's guidelines, the maximum period allowed for full adjustment is three years.

The IMF thus places almost all the responsibility for the 'adjustment' on the shoulders of the debtor nation. Creditor banks and nations are asked, at most, to provide very short term 'bridging loans' to prevent an insolvency crisis while the country 'adjusts'. The IMF's approach begs a large number of questions and creates a whole series of problems for the local economy. It assumes that no alterations can be made in the rules of the game on the international financial market. The only element in the equation that is made to 'adjust' is the country's trade balance. If the balance of payments problem faced by the developing country has been largely caused by the unexpected quadrupling of interest rates on the world market — as was the case for Latin American countries in the early 1980s — this is no concern of the Fund. In the eyes of IMF officials, the high level of world interest rates is a harsh fact of life, with which the debtor nation has got to learn to live.

This was very much the attitude taken by Jacques de Larosière, until recently managing director of the IMF, in a leaflet he published in June 1984, under the title *Does the Fund impose austerity?* [2] It is not, he argues, that the Fund spitefully imposes harsh adjustment programmes on its members. The explanation, he says, is far simpler: 'Economic adjustment is inescapable. No country can live permanently beyonds its means.' This is an international version of Margaret Thatcher's justification of monetarist policies: 'There Is No Alternative' (which gained her the nickname 'Tina' among British Labour Party politicians).

But it is poppycock. As Schlesinger has shown, the USA showed no concern for austerity during its development period, running up large deficits. And yet it managed to grow into the most powerful economy in the world. More important still, the USA refused in 1979 to 'live within its means' and cut its fiscal deficit. As we shall show later, it was the US government's decision to cover its deficit by boosting interest rates and thus attract into the country capital from all over the world that provoked the current crisis. It is only, apparently, the poor and weak developing countries that have 'no alternative' to austerity.

The IMF's assumption that no changes can be introduced into the world financial market is built into its methodology. What is important in the conventional balance of payments analysis is that the two accounts balance, that any deficit in one of the items is covered by a surplus elsewhere. Take Table 2.1, which shows Latin America's balance of payments from 1977 to 1986. It demonstrates clearly the alarming run-up to the debt crisis in the late 1970s and early 1980s, when increasingly large loans had to be raised abroad to cover the current account deficit, which was spiralling out of control. Finally, in 1982, the crisis exploded: the current account deficit remained very high, but foreign borrowing collapsed. The region ran an unprecedented balance of payments deficit, of $20.4 billion, equivalent to 3 per cent of the region's total economic output.

The table suggests that the situation has improved dramatically since then. Largely because of the efficacy of the IMF adjustment programmes, the huge balance of payments deficit was transformed into a surplus in just two years. A remarkable recovery.

But is this the full story? Is this table as objective and value-free as it seems? We do not think so. First of all, the organisation of the balance is not rational. Payment of interest and dividends, which are capital items, are not included in the capital account, as one would expect, but are found, together with freight, insurance and foreign travel, in the service section of the current account. There is a very simple reason for this anomaly (though not one that is often mentioned): it helps to prevent a country placing restrictions on the remittance of profits and interest. In the agreement it signs with the IMF over the convertibility of its currency, a country commits itself to not placing restrictions on service payments.

But this is only a detail — though it is one that illustrates clearly the IMF's priorities. It is far more important to ask whether or not this arrangement of the data provides an accurate yardstick for assessing Latin America's external sector from a regional point of view. Does it measure the net result of the flow of foreign resources in and out of the region? Does it tell us whether Latin America is receiving more hard currency than it sends out, or whether, on the contrary, it is being drained of resources? It is this relation — the net flow of resources — that is crucial to Latin America.

It is evident that the conventional balance of payments table does not measure this. What it tells us is whether or not Latin America is managing to pay its bills to its external creditors. It is a table drawn up with the interests of the creditor banks and governments very much in mind. But, from a Latin American perspective, what is important is not so much 'whether' as 'how'. If Latin America is paying its bills because interest rates have fallen, then it is fine, because the region is not suffering. But if these bills are being paid only through a drastic reduction in imports, then it is bad news, because living standards are being eroded to make these payments.

An alternative balance of payments

This aspect of the foreign accounts is shown in Table 2.2, which shows net capital flows in and out of the region. It is the real thermometer that measures the health of Latin America's external sector. And the story told by Table 2.2 is very different from the tale recounted in Table 2.1. It suggests that, far from the crisis being over for Latin America, it has stabilised at a dangerous level. In 1983, 1984 and 1985, Latin America was forced to send abroad each year, in net terms, over $30 billion, about 5 per cent of economic output. It is this that is the root cause of the 'de-development'.

Both of these two very different approaches are important. Latin American countries cannot be concerned merely with the net balance of resources, in and out of the region; they also need to consider the demands of foreign creditors. But what is wrong is that the IMF takes into account only the interests of the creditors. The health of the financial market is given absolute priority over the well-being of ordinary Latin Americans.

This clash of views has interesting consequences for language. Take the term 'adjustment', with its implication of harmonious equilibrium. For the IMF, the Latin American economy is 'adjusted' when it is able to honour all its external

Table 2.1
Latin America: balance of payments ($ bn)

	1977	78	79	80	81	82	83	84	85	86
Current account										
trade balance (A)	2.9	−2.6	0.1	−1.4	−1.7	9.1	31.5	38.7	34.3	18.0
services (net) (B)	−11.9	−15.3	−21.7	−29.3	−41.4	−47.4	−40.3	−40.9	−38.0	−34.7
balance (C = A + B)	−9.0	−17.9	−21.6	−30.7	−41.3	−38.3	−8.8	−2.2	−3.7	−16.7
Capital account										
foreign investment (D)	3.0	3.9	5.0	5.7	7.5	5.4	3.1	3.4	4.0	4.0†
loans (E)	28.0	51.0	54.0	62.1	77.8	64.0	40.3	27.7	23.6	31.5
amortisation* (F)	−11.7	−17.4	−23.0	−21.5	−22.6	−23.3	−14.7	−14.5	−13.5	−15.2
other flows** (G)	−4.7	−11.6	−5.3	−13.2	−21.8	−28.2	−25.6	−8.1	−10.1	−11.6
balance (H=D+E+F+G)	14.6	25.9	30.7	33.1	40.9	17.9	3.1	8.5	4.0	8.7
Overall balance (I=H+C)	5.6	8.0	9.1	2.4	−0.4	−20.4	−5.7	6.3	0.3	−8.0
Net change in reserves*	−5.6	−8.0	−9.1	−2.4	0.4	20.4	5.7	−6.3	−0.3	8.0

*   It covers amortisation of all long and medium-term public and publicly-guaranteed debt, and private debt when available.
**   This figure is residual. It has been calculated by taking the annual influx (loans and foreign investments), deducting the outflow (net services and amortisation) and taking into account other registered capital movements (trade balance and net change in reserves). As a residue, it will include net fluctuations in short-term debt and all non-registered capital movements, such as capital flight, non-registered trade and errors and omissions.
***   A minus sign indicates an increase in reserves.
†   our estimate

Sources: 1. IDB reports; 2. Calculated from ECLAC's annual figures for gross foreign debt and the World Bank's amortisation figures; 3. World Debt Tables, World Bank.

commitments. It was thus satisfactorily 'adjusted' in both 1984 and 1985 (*see* Table 2.1). But, in the approach reflected in Table 2.2, these were precisely the years of greatest 'maladjustment', when the external squeeze was harshest. From this perspective, the economy will be 'adjusted' only when it drastically reduces debt-servicing or receives in foreign investment and foreign loans sufficient hard currency to cover its outlay on interest and dividends.

It is interesting to note that J.M. Keynes, the British economist who played a key role in the setting up of the IMF, did not share the present view of Fund officials that all, or almost all, of the 'adjustment' has to be made by the country facing balance of payments difficulties. At the Bretton Woods conference in the US in 1944, when the decision to set up both the IMF and the World Bank was taken, Keynes argued that the Fund should have the power to borrow money on a large scale from the reserves of the countries which had balance of payments surpluses and to lend it to developing countries with deficits.[3] Unlike de Larosière, he believed that if a developing country adopted astute policies it could overcome a balance of payments crisis and still grow. In his view, there was nothing inevitable in austerity.

Table 2.2
Latin America: the flow of resources
($ bn)

	1977	78	79	80	81	82	83	84	85	86
Outflow										
Net services (total)(a)	11.9	15.3	21.7	29.3	41.4	47.4	40.3	40.9	38.0	34.7
interest	6.1	8.2	14.4	18.3	27.3	36.1	31.4	36.0	34.8	30.5
others	5.8	7.1	7.3	11.0	14.1	11.3	8.9	4.9	3.2	4.2
Amortisation* (b)	11.7	17.4	23.0	21.5	22.6	23.3	14.7	14.5	13.5	15.2
Other outflows**(c)	4.7	11.6	5.3	13.2	21.8	28.2	25.6	8.1	10.1	11.6
Total (d=a+b+c)	28.3	43.3	50.0	64.0	85.8	98.9	80.6	63.5	61.6	61.5
Inflow										
Loans (e)	28.0	51.0	54.0	62.1	77.8	64.0	40.3	27.7	23.6	31.5
Foreign investment (f)	3.0	3.9	5.0	5.7	7.5	5.4	3.1	3.4	4.0	4.0†
Total(g=e+f)	31.0	54.9	59.0	67.8	85.3	69.4	43.4	31.9	27.6	35.5
Net Transfer										
(h=g−d) (h=i+j)	2.7	10.6	9.0	3.8	−0.5	−29.5	−37.2	−32.4	−34.0	−26.0
Achieved through:										
Trade balance***(i)	−2.9	2.6	−0.1	1.4	1.7	−9.1	−31.5	−38.7	−34.3	−18.0
Net change in reserves****(j)	5.6	8.0	9.1	2.4	−2.2	−20.4	−5.7	6.3	0.3	−0.8

* It covers amortisation of all long- and medium-term public and publicly-guaranteed debt, and private debt when available.

** This figure is residual. It has been calculated by taking the annual influx (loans and foreign investment), deducting the outflow (net services and amortisation) and taking into account other registered capital movements (trade balance and net change in reserves). As a residue, it will include net fluctuations in short-term debt and all non-registered capital movements, such as capital flight, non-registered trade and errors and omissions.

*** A trade surplus is represented by a minus sign, as it indicates a flow of resources out of the region.

**** A decrease in reserves is indicated by a minus sign, as it indicates a flow of resources out of the region.

† our estimate

Sources: 1. IDB annual reports; 2. ECLAC annual reports; 3. World Debt Tables, World Bank; 4. Calculated from ECLAC's annual figures for gross foreign debt and the World Bank's amortisation figures.

Largely as a result of US pressure, Keynes's proposal lost its more audacious aspects during the long negotiations. But there remained enough of the original vision for the IMF to establish as one of its objectives:

> To facilitate the expansion and balanced growth of international trade and to contribute thereby to the promotion and maintenance of high levels of employment and real income and the development of the productive resources of all members as primary objectives of economic policy.

Show that to a Latin American finance minister and wait for the sarcastic comments!

The IMF and Latin America

After a phase of great activity in the 1950s and 1960s, the IMF declined in importance on the world stage, as it was rendered almost irrelevant by the combined impact of the refusal of the great capitalist powers to find a global solution to the dollar crisis, their disregard for Bretton Woods rules and the increased tension between the two superpowers.[4] Even the resources it handled lost significance, falling from 16.2 per cent of world trade in 1945 to 8.2 per cent in 1972 and 4.3 per cent in 1978.

The Latin American debt crisis let to a dramatic reversal of this trend, for the IMF appeared to the banks like a godsend. The banks were delighted by the profits they made from the first rescheduling in 1982, in which the panic-stricken Mexicans agreed to highly unfavourable conditions. But they were terrified that, in the succession of Latin American reschedulings that they began to realise was inevitable, neither they nor the governments in the industrialised countries would be able to force the Latin American nations to impose the harsh policies needed to extract the large trade surpluses necessary to finance debt-servicing payments in hard currency. During a visit to Buenos Aires, Karl Otto Poehl, IMF governor for West Germany, was quite open about this: 'The IMF is our only hope. It is the only institution that can lend money and impose conditions for doing so. No government can do this, nor any bank.'[5]

Latin America's view of the IMF

However, betrayal of its origins is not the only charge that Latin American economists have brought against the IMF. They also claim that, even if you accept its basic premise that each debtor nation has to carry out, single-handedly, the whole of the adjustment, its policies are misguided and inefficient. In the first place, IMF policies can only work, within their limited objective of reducing external payments deficits, if they are applied in isolated fashion by one or two countries. Once a large number of countries starts to apply them, the whole process becomes self-defeating. This is because the IMF assumes that a debtor nation can savagely reduce its imports while maintaining its exports at the previous level. But it is obvious that, if numerous countries cut back on imports simultaneously, then the level of world trade will fall. The debtor country will be very hard-pressed to maintain its exports at their previous level, let alone increase them. Moreover, world prices will drop with the increased competition, so that the same volume of exports will bring in lower earnings. To achieve the planned trade surplus, the debtor country has to cut back imports even further, which worsens the local recession and adds to the stagnation of world trade. . . The whole process can quickly become a vicious circle, as Latin America's experience in the last few years has clearly demonstrated.

In the second place, IMF policies, which are formulated with the basic objective of producing dollars for debt-servicing, unleash a series of unpleasant economic forces on the domestic economy which become extremely difficult to control. Though experience has varied from Latin American country to Latin American country, the basic mechanism in each has been similar. In its adjustment programme, the IMF insists on two parallel lines of action, both geared to slashing the current account deficit. Firstly, it insists on a reduction in consumer demand, as this demand feeds imports either directly through increased demand for imported consumer goods or indirectly through additional demand for imported machinery or raw materials so that domestic production can be increased. In practice, this means a big reduction in government spending, which inevitably leads to recession. And secondly, local production has to be channelled away from the domestic market into exports. In practice, this means the devaluation of the local currency, so that locally produced goods become cheaper on the world market.

The main complaint by Latin American economists is that these measures have created a new monster, 'hyperstagflation', that is, violent recession combined with a very high rate of inflation. The impact on the local economies was so severe that even such a conservative observer as Henry Kissinger commented that 'the cure is worse than the disease'.

These policies have been only partially effective. Though some Latin American currencies had become absurdly overvalued by the early 1980s, the devaluation by itself rarely proved sufficient to boost export earnings. This is partly because many Latin American countries are dependent on commodity exports, which are generally priced in dollars and thus not affected by the devaluation of the local currency, and partly because of the stagnation in world trade, exacerbated by the IMF's own policies. Throughout Latin America, the most effective policy for reducing the current account deficit was the reduction in imports, which was precisely the measure with the most harmful impact on the local economy.

Feeding inflation

There are three principal ways in which inflation increased. The first — and by far the simplest — was the impact of more expensive imported goods on the cost-of-living index. It is evident that this impact was greater for economies that were heavily dependent on imported goods, which, as we have seen, tended to be the smaller countries. The second inflationary pressure stemmed from the nature of much of the region's foreign debt. Many of the loans were contracted to service old loans and, of the limited amount that actually entered the region, very little was used to finance productive activities that would quickly produce the dollars required for debt-servicing. As we shall see in Chapter 8, the loans were used in Chile to finance the expansion of new economic groups, which grew very rapidly, largely as the result of speculative investment in property. In Argentina, the country where capital flight was most rife, many of the loans went to a small group of privileged companies, including multinationals, who immediately deposited them in bank accounts in the industrialised countries. In Brazil, a much larger proportion of the loans went into productive activities, but even here there were difficulties. Some of the ventures, like the gaint Açominas steel mill, were over-dimensioned, with a long maturity period and an uncertain export market. Others, such as road-building schemes and the programme for producing alcohol from sugar-cane, did not really require foreign funding.

In 1982 and 1983, when the Latin American governments finally tried to sort out the chaotic aftermath of the debt crisis, they found that few of the companies that had originally contracted the debts, whether state-owned or private, were in a position to service them. Unable to borrow more money abroad, they simply had no hard currency which they could use. Though at that time both the Reagan and the Thatcher governments were highly critical of state interference in the economy and expressed great confidence in the 'magic of the market-place', they were the first to press the Latin American governments to take over responsibility for all the loans, whether or not they had been contracted with a government guarantee originally. In the end, almost all governments allowed themselves to be saddled with the knotty question of debt-servicing, though they received no concession from the banks in return. Chile, in particular, lost a unique opportunity, because, unusually for a Latin American borrower, most of its debt did not have a government guarantee. And the problem was not just raising the dollars to pay the interest — which might have been thought enough of a difficulty in itself — but also limiting the damage to the local economy, particularly the inflationary impact.

The mechanism at work is relatively simple. In most Latin American countries (except the oil exporters), private companies dominate exports, which usually come from the mining, farming and industrial sectors. These companies, which contracted only a small part of the foreign debt, send off their exports, deposit their dollars with the central bank and then, quite naturally, expect payment in local currency. The situation of the big state-owned oil companies is basically similar, for, though they belong to the government, these firms need to make profits just like private companies. Ideally, the companies that originally took out the foreign loans should buy these dollars, paying the market price in local currency. This would cause minimal disruption to the local economy, for it would mean that approximately the same amount of local currency would be taken out of the money supply as is put into it.

However, this rarely happens, for few of the indebted companies have the money to buy the dollars. This means that, if the debtor government wants to avoid default, it must itself both service the debts and take over responsibility for paying the exporters. No Latin American government can possibly find these resources from its normal budget funds, which are always inadequate for routine needs. It has, basically, three options: it can cut back public spending; it can print more money;

or it can raise money on the local money market through the sale of federal bonds. The first two measures have clear disadvantages. Public spending in most Latin American countries has already been cut to the bone and further reductions would be most unpopular. The printing of money is highly inflationary. For this reason, governments have tended to opt for the third measure — the issue of federal bonds — as the least damaging, politically or economically. But this option, too, has serious disadvantages. It sets in motion an internal debt snowball, almost as alarming as the foreign one. The amount of money that the government needs to raise increases continuously, as it has to find resources not only to pay exporters, but also to pay interest on the bonds it has issued in the past. This ever-expanding demand pushes up interest rates; this, in turn, puts up the cost of servicing the old debt, increases inflation and discourages investment. . . The whole 'stagflationary' process becomes a spiral from which it is difficult to escape.

The third inflationary pressure is more structural. Under normal conditions, there is an approximate balance between supply and demand, as the availability of goods and services on the market is related to the price that is paid for them. If a commodity is in short supply, the market ensures that its price rises, thus attracting other producers and increasing the supply. The existence of monopolies and oligopolies means that the price mechanism in practice is far less effective than the textbooks suggest, but it has proved, as yet, the most effective mediator between supply and demand.

However, the current heavy debt-servicing, with the net transfer of resources out of the country, upsets this balance. The exporter sends goods abroad, receiving dollars in exchange. But, instead of these dollars being used to increase imports and thus to maintain, approximately, the balance on the local market, the dollars too are exported. The Latin American country gets neither the goods nor the dollars. The exporter is paid in local currency, but there is no equivalent product, either produced locally or imported, for him to purchase. A larger amount of money is chasing the same amount of goods, so a third inflationary pressure is inevitably generated.

The whole syndrome is reminiscent of the inflation that emerged in the Weimar Republic between 1919 and 1923 because of the heavy war reparations that Germany was making. It was only once the economy collapsed, after slipping into an uncontrollable spiral of hyperinflation, that the Allies agreed to the full renegotiation of the country's debts that relieved most of the pressure.

An inflationary spiral can be checked by tough measures, firmly enforced. This has been demonstrated by the 'new economic plan' carried out by the Paz Estenssoro government in Bolivia in 1985, by the Austral Plan carried out by Raúl Alfonsín in Argentina the same year, and by the Cruzado Plan carried out by José Sarney in Brazil in 1986. These plans have varied considerably, particularly with respect to the social cost they have entailed. It is by no means surprising, perhaps, that the IMF has shown greatest enthusiasm for the Bolivian plan, which was precisely the one that created the most savage cut in the purchasing power of wages — a remarkable 67 per cent decline in the six months after the announcement of the plan. The Brazilian plan, which actually improved living standards, was carried out without any IMF involvement, and it is highly unlikely that the IMF would have given its stamp of approval if it had been asked.

But none of these plans really faced up to the built-in inflationary pressure stemming from the heavy debt-servicing. In the Bolivian case, a breathing space was created by the extraordinary decline in domestic demand as a result of the fall in wages. In the case of both Argentina and Brazil, the impact was temporarily repressed by the wide-ranging price freeze imposed by the governments. But, as both these countries are discovering, the inflationary pressure immediately re-emerges once any move is made to loosen the freeze. Many Latin American economists now believe that inflation will be decisively defeated only after real relief from debt-servicing has been achieved.

Debt-induced recession

The other by-product of the IMF's adjustment programmes that has come under mounting criticism in Latin America is the recession itself. Deliberately provoked in the beginning to reduce demand for imported goods and to bring down the governments' deficits, the recession has gained its own self-sustaining momentum, becoming difficult to reverse. With rising inflation, wages have progressively lost their purchasing power and demand has fallen yet further. Sorely afflicted by the combined impact of increased costs and falling demand, manufacturers have reduced output and sacked workers. Demand has fallen even more, deepening the recession yet further. The vicious circle can be broken, as Brazil has demonstrated dramatically, but in the medium term such action becomes incompatible with full debt-servicing.

For the people of Latin America, the recession is nonsense. It is absurd for factories to be operating with high levels of idle capacity when underemployment and underconsumption are serious social problems. It is ridiculous to be reducing the slice of the economic cake available to each inhabitant precisely when a sizeable portion, of fixed dimensions, has to be sent abroad each year. If the economy were growing rapidly, then the piece that has to be sent abroad would become progressively smaller relative to the overall size of the cake.

This can be illustrated by a quick calculation. From 1980 to 1985, per capita GDP fell by 8.9 per cent. If, instead, it had grown by 10 per cent during this period, regional output would have increased by about $120 billion, instead of by about $15 billion. Apart from all the other benefits that this would have brought, it would have meant that the ratio of interest payments to the region's economic output would have been 4.5 per cent during this period, somewhat more manageable than their actual ratio of 5.4 per cent. The recession is thus, to use the economists' jargon, an 'inefficient' way of eliminating balance of payments deficits. In other words, many economic resources are wasted for each small improvement in the external accounts. From a global viewpoint, it is an irrational solution.

But, with its predatory use of natural resources and its lack of concern for the common good, capitalism is an irrational system, in which the short-term interests of powerful groups generally dominate. It is thus, perhaps, scarcely surprising that the IMF, dominated as it is by the governments and banks in the industrialised countries, should have shown little concern for the social cost of its policies, particularly as those most affected were the Latin American people, who represented no direct threat to these groups.

It was not, however, just the Latin Americans who were hurt. US exports to Latin America fell by $14 billion between 1980 and 1983. According to US Senator Bill Bradley, this led to the loss of 800,000 jobs, as well as a fall in profits. If the adjustment imposed by the IMF had allowed Latin America to grow, imports would have increased, or, at least, not fallen. Debt-servicing payments would have declined but, in compensation, jobs would have been saved both in Latin America and, to a lesser degree, in the industrialised countries. But such a solution would have demanded imagination and a willingness on the part of the banks and governments in the industrialised countries to bear part of the burden. These qualities were not forthcoming. Recession was the only way in which the debt crisis could be temporarily resolved with minimal direct costs to the governments and banks in the industrialised nations. It was rational within the overall irrationality of a system in which the interests of a few are allowed to dominate over those of the majority.

Notes

1. *Financial Times*, 23 September 1983.
2. *Does the IMF impose austerity?*, (IMF leaflet, 1984).
3. *The Poverty Brokers*, (Latin America Bureau, London, 1983) p.20.
4. Samuel Lichenstein, 'Deudas y Desarrollo en América Latina', (mimeographed paper at conference on Latin American debt at UNICAMP university, Campinas, Brazil, 1985) p. 43.
5. *Clarín*, 22 November 1983, quoted by Lichenstein, op.cit.
6. Peter Körner, Gero Maass, Thomas Siebold, Rainer Tetzlaff, *The IMF and the Debt Crisis* (Zed Books, London, 1986).

3. The Human Cost of the Debt Crisis

Millions of abandoned children, millions of unemployed, some of the lowest wages on earth — that is what the debt crisis has meant for Latin America

There's no doubt that the Mexicans could pay off their debt, but they'd rather that the US tax-payer did. Brazil could do the same. There's enormous wealth in Mato Grosso. They could give us part of that. It's the same in Africa. It's rich up to its eyebrows.
Sir Alan Walters, leading aide to the British government, in the *Sunday Times*, 25 September 1983

The global statistics for the current recession suggest that Latin America has been through the most serious economic setback in its history. But even these figures — a 9 per cent fall in per capita economic output and a 20 per cent fall in the per capita output consumed or invested within the region (*see* Table 1.1, p.3) — are deceptive. They are averages and suggest, misleadingly, that the cost of the recession was shared equally throughout society.

But this is obviously nonsense. It is evident that the elites, with their close links with the international financial market and their opportunities for capital flight, have suffered very little and, in some cases, have actually grown richer as the result of the crisis. The brunt of the suffering has been borne by the poor. At the beginning of 1986, at least 150 million Latin Americans, two-fifths of the total population of 385 million, were believed to be living below the poverty line. Five years earlier, the number had been put at 130 million.[1] Two factors — one structural and the other conjunctural — have accounted for the particular vulnerability of the very poor: their position in the employment structure; and the impact of particular government policies. Let us look more closely at these two influences.

The vulnerability of the poor

During the 1960s and 1970s, Latin America experienced a rapid process of urbanisation of both 'pull' and 'push' varieties. People flocked to the cities in search of jobs in industry (the 'pull'), and were turned off the land with the expansion of the agricultural frontier and the mechanisation of farming (the 'push'). In 1984, 69 per cent of Latin America's population lived in towns or cities, compared with 49 per cent in 1960. Most of the migrants were unskilled. They got jobs wherever they could, mainly on building sites.

With this intense urbanisation, agriculture lost its old prominence, with its share in the region's gross domestic product falling from 17 per cent in 1960 to 12 per cent in 1980. Industry and services expanded rapidly, but they could not absorb the huge influx of labour. It was estimated in 1980, before the recession hit the region, that about 30–34 million people, about 28 per cent of the labour force, were unemployed or underemployed.[2] Because of the relatively high population growth rate, the Latin American economy needed to expand by 5−6 per cent just to stop the situation from getting worse. It meant that the two biggest countries, Brazil and Mexico, had to create each year 1.4 million and 1 million new jobs, respectively.

At the best of times, a Latin American construction worker has a precarious life, for he is employed for irregular periods and has no job security. But when recession hits the region, he is particularly defenceless. The government reduces public works, and the construction industry is immediately affected, long before sectors geared to exports. Large numbers of workers are sacked. White-collar workers — and executives — also lose their jobs, but the unskilled tend to be the first to go.

During periods of high economic growth, the standard of living of construction workers may be higher in the cities than if they had remained in the countryside as subsistence peasant farmers, but, during periods of recession, the opposite is true. In the cities, they need money for everything — rent, food, electricity, water and so on. A money wage is essential. In the countryside, those with access to land (admittedly, a declining proportion) can at least produce their own food and are far less vulnerable to malnutrition than the underemployed in the cities.

Most workers who lose their jobs do not become unemployed in the way that this term is used in the industrialised countries. Without unemployment benefit, they would starve if they stopped work completely. They have to find some form of employment, however pitiful. Statistical methods could be devised to measure underemployment accurately, but most governments, reluctant to face up to the full scale of the social crisis, have not developed them. As a result, the existing unemployment figures seriously underestimate the problem, but they give an idea of the tendency in recent years (*see* Figure 3.1).

There is also another, more subtle, structural mechanism at work. Income is distributed very unequally in Latin America, far more unjustly than in most other regions of the world. World Bank statistics[3] show that in several Latin American countries the richest 10 per cent of the population account for over 40 per cent of national income. The worst case is Brazil: it is the only country in the World Bank's table in which the richest tenth take more than half of the income (50.6 per cent). As is perhaps to be expected, it is the very poor who lose out. Three Latin American countries vie for the smallest share of national income going to the poorest 20 per cent: Peru (1.9 per cent), Brazil (2 per cent) and Panama (2 per cent). (In Britain, by no means the most egalitarian of countries, World Bank figures suggest that the richest 10 per cent take 23.4 per cent of income, while the poorest 20 per cent have 7 per cent.)

During periods of recession, the rich are always efficient in defending their share of the cake. Employers reduce their labour force or cut wages to protect profit margins. Big economic groups generally have access to the government and can ensure that their interests are not seriously harmed by the austerity measures. The rich can also limit the extent to which high inflation erodes their incomes, and perhaps even benefit from the difficulties experienced by other sectors. They can speculate on the local money market, where interest rates have been spectacularly

Figure 3.1
Latin America: Unemployment
(average annual rates)
(% of labour force)

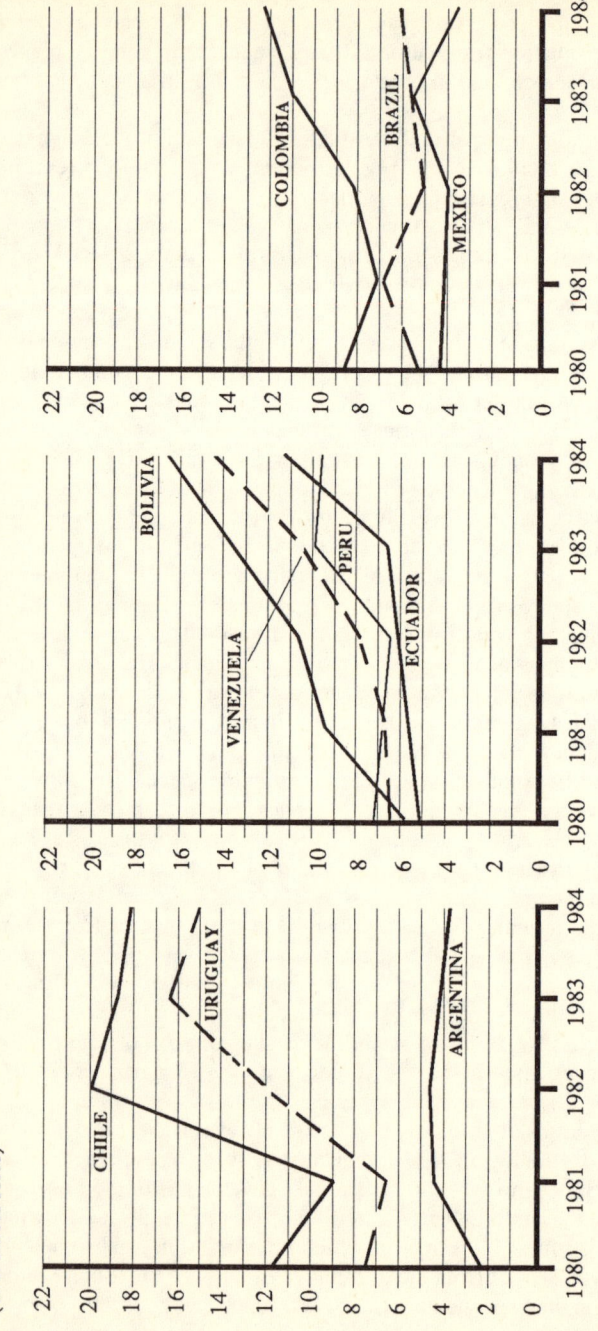

The figures are based on a sample of towns and regions in each country selected by ECLAC as together being representative of the national situation.
Source: ECLAC, based on official information.

high in much of Latin America as the hard-pressed governments sell bonds to service the internal debt. They can invest in assets, such as property, which maintain their value. They can indulge in capital flight, keeping part of their assets in hard currency. And so on.

None of these mechanisms is available to workers. As a result of the high inflation, the value of their wages is rapidly eroded and they, involuntarily, transfer a part of their income to their bosses, suffering a disproportionately large share of the fall in living standards as a result. Life becomes a daily struggle, but it is difficult for them to fight back. It requires considerable mobilisation to convince the government to allow more frequent wage rises, and this is a hard task when unemployment is rising. Even in countries where the government is relatively sympathetic to workers' demands, finance ministers are understandably reluctant to allow quarterly — or monthly — increases, because of the risk of hyperinflation. Moreover, there is always a long time lag before any compensatory measure is taken.

The vulnerability of the poor, created by the particularly unequal form of capitalist expansion in Latin America, has been exacerbated by short-term measures, first taken by Latin American governments to try and avert the debt crisis, and then imposed by the IMF in its endeavour to resolve the debt-servicing problem within the region.

In the run-up to the debt crisis, many Latin American countries created generous incentives for export crops in an attempt to boost dollar earnings. The neglect of food crops destined for local consumption spread in 1982 and 1983, as the IMF insisted on drastic cuts in the subsidies for farm credit. In most countries, the production of food crops stopped rising or even fell, leading to shortages and big price increases. The most spectacular case was probably Brazil: the farming area planted with export crops tripled between 1970 and 1985, going from 5.6 million hectares to 17.1 million hectares; during the same period, the area planted with food crops grew only slowly, from 20.3 million hectares to 24.0 million hectares. As a result, per capita production of foodstuffs for local consumption fell from 557.2 kgs in 1970 to 424.9 kgs in 1985, and food prices rose far more quickly than other items in the cost-of-living index. As is discussed more fully later in this chapter, malnutrition, particularly among children, became a serious social problem in Brazil for the first time ever.

As part of their 'adjustment' programmes, governments have also been forced to cut back sharply in public services, particularly health and education, upon which the poor, but not the rich, depend. In some countries, the deterioration has been particularly painful, for it has followed a period of military rule during which the outlay on public services was deliberately reduced so as to free more resources for investment in industry. In Chile, per capita public expenditure on social services fell by about 20 per cent between 1974 and 1984.[4] Even in Brazil, where the outlay on health increased from 2.5 per cent of GDP in 1975 to 4.0 per cent in 1980, the system tended to care almost exclusively for registered workers whose well-being was essential for industrial development. It provided greatly inferior services for the growing mass of unregistered workers, particularly in the countryside.

This adds up to a bleak picture for the poor, even those with jobs. In Mexico, the real minimum wage fell by 35 per cent between 1981 and 1983.[5] In Peru, the real average wage for unskilled workers dropped by 60 per cent between 1979 and 1984.[6] In Brazil, the average real income fell by 14 per cent between 1979 and 1984.[7] By 1985, about 52 million people — some 40 per cent of the Brazilian population — were living in absolute poverty, with a monthly income of $35 or less. With so many Latin Americans now living in urban areas and thus dependent on a money income for survival, it seems remarkable that they have coped at all. How have they managed it?

Survival mechanisms

The main survival mechanism has been the so-called 'informal' sector — the huge underworld of unregistered economic activities that has been created by workers forced to find a livelihood outside the system. With no dole or social welfare, sacked workers have joined the mass of street vendors, rubbish dump scavengers and old newspaper tradesmen who are found today in all of Latin America's cities. These informal sectors have been growing all over the continent. In Brazil, the proportion of the urban workforce employed in the informal sector was estimated to have risen from 27 per cent in 1980 to 37 per cent in 1985.[8] This meant that by 1985 there were 13 million people scratching out a living in the cities from some form of marginal employment.

However, as is perhaps to be expected, these informal activities are most developed in the smaller economies that have been most hurt by the recession. In Peru, almost half the labour force is estimated by the government to be working in the informal sector. Hernando de Soto, a Peruvian economist, believes that illegal cottage industries supply as much as 90 per cent of all clothing manufactured in the country. In Bolivia, the country that has suffered most severely of all from the recession, the informal sector is even larger. Its output is believed to be about the same size as — or even slightly larger than — that of the formal economy. It is an indication of the doggedness with which people have struggled to earn enough to support their families, against desperate odds.

By far the most publicised activity in the Bolivian informal sector is the cultivation and trading of coca, the bush from whose leaves cocaine is extracted. Until mid-1986, about 160,000 tonnes of coca leaves were produced each year, chiefly in the Chaparé region near Cochabamba. About one-tenth was sold to local people, who chew it to dull hunger or use it to make tea to combat altitude sickness. The rest was smuggled abroad, either as coca paste or as cocaine sulphate, the semi-refined product. These illegal exports brought in each year $2.5−3 billion, according to the Bolivian government, or $4 billion, according to US authorities. They were worth five or six times the value of legal exports.

In July 1986, the Paz Estenssoro government, with the aid of the Bolivian armed forces and several hundred specially-trained US troops, began a tough drive against the coca planters. Though no deal was officially announced, it was evident that the Reagan administration had intervened, making its support for Bolivia's efforts to reschedule its foreign debt and to obtain World Bank loans conditional on a much more serious attempt to eradicate the coca plantations, which supply much of the raw material for the cocaine trade in the US.

In the short term, the drive has been successful, drastically reducing production. But most of the repression has been directed against the small producers, not the cocaine barons. Men such as Roberto Suarez, who once boasted that he could single-handedly pay off Bolivia's foreign debt of $3 billion, may decide to lie low for a few months, but their power is not readily broken. And the several hundred thousand small farmers who used to earn their living from the cultivation of coca must be suffering severely. As the government has done little to encourage them to move into other crops, it is likely that most will revert to coca as soon as the repression is lifted.

Even when it is operating freely, the coca trade has only a tiny multiplier effect on the rest of the economy. This is partly because it is an unregistered activity, so the profits are not 'socialised' through taxation, and partly because earnings are concentrated in the hands of a tiny elite, which indulges in conspicuous consumption, largely of imported goods, and thus makes only a very small contribution to domestic demand. As James Dunkerley has pointed out, the cocaine trade has all the characteristics of a free-zone enclave, which takes advantage of the local cheap labour but does little to promote the long-term economic development of the region.[9]

Though it is the most profitable activity in the informal sector, the cocaine trade is not the biggest employer. Many more people work in small, unregistered businesses in the commercial and service sectors. A survey carried out in 1977 showed that already half of the labour force in La Paz was working illegally. With the marked deterioration in the economy since then, the proportion must be much higher today. Moreover, the very violence of the recession has forced people to invent new, hybrid forms of labour in which activities in both the formal and the informal sectors are combined. In the five months following the introduction of Victor Paz Estenssoro's stabilisation plan in August 1985, the real value of wages fell by 67 per cent. This came after four turbulent years in which per capita income had dropped by 30 per cent. By early 1986, a primary school teacher in an urban area was spending four-fifths of her wage on transport to and from school.

The monthly minimum wage did not cover the cost of even the first ten items in the family food basket, let alone rent, transport, household bills, health expenditure and so on. As a result, many in the relatively privileged group of workers to have a job in the formal economy were also resorting to other activities in the informal sector. Factory workers were using holidays or sick leave to make a quick trip to Santiago in neighbouring Chile to smuggle back consumer goods in short supply in Bolivia. Civil servants were trading in dollars on the black market during their lunch hours. And so on.

The government is seriously hampered by a large informal sector. It is deprived of much-needed revenue, as no taxes are paid on these irregular activities. Its capacity to administer the economy effectively is also undermined, with so many activities outside its control. Many people, once established in the informal sector, may be loath to revert to the formal economy once the crisis ends. The informal sector has helped people survive, but it has not provided them with an adequate income. As a result, standards of health and nutrition among the poorer sectors of the population, already very low before the crisis, have fallen yet further. It was estimated that, in 1970, there were about 50 million people in Latin America and the Caribbean who were under the absolute poverty line, that is, whose incomes would not cover basic needs. There were another 60 million people, who were believed to be under the poverty line, that is, whose incomes were less than twice that considered essential to cover basic needs. In all, about 35 per cent of the region's population was thought to be undernourished, or in serious danger of becoming undernourished.[10] Though the supply of major foodstuffs increased during the 1970s, it did not keep up with population growth. By 1981, about 130 million people — 37 per cent of the total population — were estimated to live below the poverty line.[11] From 1981 to 1984, the supply of major foodstuffs actually fell, by 2.5 per cent. As the population continued to grow each year, by about 2.4 per cent, undernourishment must have risen considerably. As the report itself concludes, its estimate, of 150 million people under the poverty line in 1986, is probably an underestimate.

Serious health problems

Undernourishment in Latin America has been exacerbated by the debt crisis, but it cannot be considered to have been caused by it. One of the most striking characteristics of the Latin American continent is the seriousness of its health problems in the light of its level of economic development. Per capita economic output in the ten Latin American countries with the largest foreign debts varies from $540 in Bolivia to $3,410 in Venezuela. It is not high when compared with the USA ($15,390) or the United Kingdom ($8,570), but it is considerably higher than in most other developing countries, such as China ($310) or Uganda ($230).

Yet, in four of the ten Latin American countries, the daily per capita supply of calories, that is, what the average person eats each day, is less than that required for a healthy life (*see* Table 3.1). As the upper and middle sectors consume far more than their share, these statistics suggest that a sizeable proportion of the overall population in these four countries is seriously undernourished. Yet, from the level of their per capita output, these countries should have had the resources to eliminate this problem. China, Senegal, Uganda and Burma — four other developing countries, chosen randomly — appear, from the figures, to face less serious problems of undernourishment among their populations, though they have much lower per capita economic output. It seems remarkable that Burma, with a per capita output that is just a twentieth of Venezuela's, appears to have a less serious problem of undernourishment.

Similarly, infant mortality rates in all but two (Chile and Uruguay) of the Latin American countries are much higher than might be expected from the per capita economic output. Again, it is remarkable that China, with a much lower per capita economic output, has a lower level of infant mortality than six of the ten Latin American countries.

Table 3.1
Social indicators for Latin America and other countries

	GNP per capita	Daily calorie supply per capita		Infant Mortality 1984
	($ 1984)	Total 1983	As % of requirement*	
Latin America				
Venezuela	3,410	2,451	99	38
Argentina	2,230	3,159	119	34
Mexico	2,040	2,934	126	51
Uruguay	1,980	2,647	99	29
Brazil	1,720	2,533	106	68
Chile	1,700	2,574	105	22
Colombia	1,390	2,546	110	48
Ecuador	1,150	2,043	89	67
Peru	1,000	1,997	85	95
Bolivia	540	1,954	82	118
Other developing countries				
Senegal	380	2,436	102	138
China	310	2,620	111	36
Uganda	230	2,351	101	110
Burma	180	2,534	117	67
Industrialised countries				
United States	15,390	3,623	137	11
United Kingdom	8,570	3,226	128	10

* The daily calorie requirement per capita refers to the calories needed to sustain a person at normal levels of activity and health, taking into account age and sex distributions, average body weights, and environmental temperatures. For this reason, it will vary from country to country.

Source: *World Development Report*, 1986, The World Bank

It is evident that the very unequal distribution of income throughout most of Latin America is responsible for these anomalies. Many Latin American economies are bigger and more powerful than those in most of the rest of the developing world, yet so much of the wealth is concentrated in the hands of a few that the poor are no better off than elsewhere. This is clearly illustrated in the pitiful state of so many children in Brazil, Latin America's largest and most industrialised economy.

Brazil's 'abandoned' children

Even at the height of the so-called Brazilian 'economic miracle' in the late 1960s and early 1970s, wages for unskilled workers were low. As a result, a comparative study, carried out in 1968–70, showed malnutrition to be the underlying or associated cause of infant mortality in a large proportion of deaths in four Brazilian towns — Recife (39.0 per cent), Ribeirão Bonito (29.1 per cent), Franca (32.7 per cent) and São Paulo (28.1 per cent). In contrast, it accounted for relatively few deaths (though perhaps more than might be expected) in two US cities — San Francisco (3.7 per cent) and Sherbrooke (2.2 per cent).

Doctor Dirce Maria Sigelum, from the Institute of Preventive Medicine at the São Paulo School of Medicine, recalled:[12] 'It was a shock to discover that malnutrition was the basic, or associated, cause of so many infant deaths in three places in São Paulo. We had not expected this in urban areas, not on this scale. Particularly in the "marvellous south".' (She was referring to the prosperous industrialised region around São Paulo). The doctor said that a later survey, carried out in 1974, in which she had participated, had confirmed these results: 42 per cent of children under two from families in the city of São Paulo whose per capita income was less than one minimum wage (that is, the lowest legal wage) were suffering from malnutrition; 67 per cent of children under two from families in the city of Rio de Janeiro whose per capita income was less than half a minimum wage were suffering from malnutrition.

As a result of the recession, wage levels fell sharply in the early 1980s. The number of undernourished children increased significantly. The incidence of anaemia among children under five in the state of São Paulo rose from 11.3 per cent in 1980 to 16.3 per cent in 1984. The percentage of new-born babies with a weight of less than 2.5 kilos — the minimum for a healthy baby — rose from 14.5 per cent in 1980 to 16.1 per cent in 1984. The proportion of children in São Paulo's hospitals suffering from malnutrition rose from 31.8 per cent in 1980 to 35.2 per cent in 1984. All these figures clearly reflect the fall in real wages among poorly-paid workers.

But, surprisingly, this deterioration is not reflected in the infant mortality rate. Before 1980, a close inverse correlation had been noted: when the minimum wage rose, infant mortality fell; and vice-versa. Because wage levels had inched up unevenly, infant mortality rates had shown an irregular downward trend. By 1980, the rate for São Paulo state had fallen to 87 deaths during the first year of life per thousand live births, compared with 121 in 1960.

However, despite the fall in living standards in the early 1980s, infant mortality continued to decline, reaching 41 by 1984. Another factor was interfering: the extensive programme of public sanitation that was bringing running water and sewerage to many of São Paulo's poor quarters. This had reduced by half the incidence of diarrhoea and parasites among babies, eliminating one of the immediate causes of death. But, though more are surviving, São Paulo's children may be less healthy than in the past. Some studies have suggested that, as a whole, children in Brazil have today more serious nutritional deficiencies than they had 30 years ago. It is a savage indictment of the progress that the country is said to have made since the early 1950s, with the enormous expansion of the country's industrial sector.

Apart from being subject to malnutrition, many of the children from the poorer sectors were excluded from the educational system, as the military governments, in power from 1964 to 1984, ran down investments in primary education. In 1985, it was calculated that, out of every 100 children of school age, 26 had not stepped inside a classroom. In other words, about three million children were being completely excluded from the education system. Only 12 out of the remaining 74 reached the end of primary school.

Moreover, the situation was deteriorating. It has been estimated[13] that, despite the population increase, the number of children beginning secondary school fell by 8.5 per cent between 1979 and 1984, from 3.1 million to 2.9 million. This decline is believed to have been caused partly by poor teaching and partly by the need for children to carry out some form of work so that they can contribute to the family income. By 1984, about 30 million people — 28 per cent of the population over five — was believed to be illiterate.

At the same time, a large number of children were not being properly cared for at home. Government officials speak of an enormous 36 million 'abandoned' children, or about half of the population under 18. But this figure is misleading, for it includes a wide range of problem children, from those in one-parent families to those who have genuinely been abandoned. Nonetheless, there is clearly a large group of children who are suffering real hardship. Some work in street markets during the day, but live at home. Others roam the streets, robbing — or 'carrying out a job', as they call it — when they need money. They are frequently maltreated by the corrupt São Paulo police, who often work with one gang while pursuing another.

Despite the return to democratic rule in March 1985, death squads still exist among the police. They no longer wipe out political activists, as in the early 1970s, but murder instead petty criminals, who are often young people under 18, who the police want to eliminate, but who, under Brazilian law, cannot be sent to prison. These squads are believed to have been responsible for 532 deaths in 1985, an all-time record. Other young people resort to prostitution. A survey carried out in 1985 showed that in Curitiba, a town of about one million inhabitants, no fewer than 30,000 youngsters, between 11 and 15 years old, were working as prostitutes.

Some of these people — about 400,000 all over Brazil — are interned in special institutions, which are frequently overcrowded, violent and promiscuous. Antônio Carlos Gômes da Costa, head of this service in Minas Gerais state, commented in September 1985: 'I am frequently asked why children so often run away from our institution. The answer is simple: they are driven to it by their remaining sense of self-respect and sanity.'

The debt crisis alone cannot be held responsible for the crisis among Brazil's children. It was a problem that began to emerge under the military government, largely because, despite the rapid economic growth, the country's enormous social inequalities actually increased. What the debt crisis has done is absorb resources and energies that should be used to tackle this and other urgent social problems. It has turned a highly unjust form of economic development into an intolerable one.

Notes

1. SELA, Comité de Acción para la Seguridad Alimentaria Regional, (mimeographed paper, April 1986).
2. Organisation of American States, 1986 annual report.

3. *World Development Report*, (World Bank, 1986).
4. Unicef, *The State of the World's Children* (1986).
5. CIDE, *Revista de la Economía Mexicana*, No. 5 (1984).
6. *Peru: Paths to Poverty*, (Latin America Bureau, London, 1986).
7. 'Pesquisa por Amostragem Domiciliar' — *PNAD*, from IBGE, quoted in *Folha de S. Paulo*, April 1986.
8. Ibid.
9. *New Left Review*, Jan—Feb 1986.
10. 'Dimensión de la Pobreza en América Latina', *Cuadernos de la Cepal*, 1982.
11. SALA/CASAR, *National Food Programmes in Latin America: A response to the Economic Crisis*.
12. Dirce Maria Sigulem, *Ciencia Hoje*, April 1982.
13. IBGE, *PNAD*, op. cit.

4. The Underlying Cause

A brief but necessary look at the long post-war development cycle that led Latin America into the trap of floating interest rates

> . . . In American academic thinking the majority opinion asserts that there is no such thing. In Europe, however, long wave theories go back into the 1800s. . .
>
> **Jay W. Forrester**, *The Futurist*, June 1985

How was it that Latin America became a prisoner of such an enormous foreign debt? Was it, as so many of its rulers claim, merely unlucky, the victim of a series of historical accidents? Accidents that began with the first rise in oil prices at the end of 1973, continued with the remarkable combination of recession and inflation in the two following years, and ended in 1979 with the second rise in oil prices and the explosion in interest rates?

All this happened, and in that order. But not by chance. A crisis of this scale cannot happen by chance, just as the First World War did not happen just because a prince was shot in Sarajevo, nor Nazism arise just because Hitler was a psychopath. In the same way, Latin America has not experienced the worst recession in its history just because Paul Volcker, the chairman of the US Federal Reserve Board, decided to boost US interest rates.

The successive increases in oil prices, the explosion in interest payments, the very multiplication of Latin America's debt are scenes in a greater drama: the long crisis in the US economy — the dynamic centre of world capitalism — that began to emerge in 1968. It is no coincidence that the snowballing of Latin America's debts began precisely in that year, with the debt growing exponentially, from $11.7bn in 1968 to $59.1bn, five times that size, by 1974.

When the first oil shock took place, the magazine *The Economist*, which represents international capital, had the detachment to announce the truth that everyone wanted to conceal: that it meant the end of the era of spectacular post-war capitalist growth. It wrote: 'Despite warnings of a slump on the scale of the 1930s, most people believe that the world faces no more than a short-lived recession — a year or so of no growth or perhaps marginal decline. . . But the world economic system, like an aeroplane in flight, can only slow down so far before it stalls and plummets to earth.'[1]

Strangely enough, as this prediction was confirmed, less and less was said about the underlying crisis, even in *The Economist*. The ruling classes handle serious crises like some families deal with a relative dying from cancer: the illness itself is never mentioned. But the crisis has lasted for two decades, if in muted form. Today it is becoming clear that what has been happening to the US economy, and by extension to the other economies in the capitalist world, has not been a series of recessions, but a prolonged depression, the cost of which has been transferred almost entirely to the periphery, particularly Latin America. It is, it would seem, one of those depressions that every 50 or so years — with a strange regularity, as if they were a curse — afflict the central engines of the capitalist economy. It is called the 'long wave' theory.

The 'long-wave' theory

Long waves are both fascinating and mysterious. They can be seen as a long symmetrical wave, in which the upward and the downward phases each last about 25 years. It is perhaps this regularity that fascinates some economists, but provokes scorn in others, particularly Americans. In the upward phases, the gross domestic product of the main capitalist economy grows by about 5 per cent a year and crises are superficial and short. But, in the 25 years of the downward phase, the recessions are long and deep, with only ephemeral recoveries, and the growth rate falls heavily.[2] In this phase, conflicts between nations and classes become more intense, favouring the outbreak of wars and revolutions (*see* Table 4.1). These symptoms have been evident since 1968, with the dollar crisis and the political upheavals of that year, and have helped to revive interest in the half-abandoned theory of the long waves. Since then average annual growth in the US has been 2.5 per cent, compared with 5.2 per cent during the upward phase, from 1940 to 1967.

What causes the long wave? Economists agree that technological innovations and the opening of new markets have been determining factors in the expansionary phases, with each one being characterised by a predominant form of accumulation of profit and investment (*see* Table 4.1). Thus the industrial revolution sparked off the expansionary cycle of 1792 to 1819, and the construction of railways throughout the world sustained the following expansion, from 1841 to 1871. The great post-war cycle, that is now in crisis, was led by the transnationals and, according to W.W. Rostow, had

> 'two main pillars in the advanced industrialised world: the diffusion of the automobile, durable consumer goods, and the life of suburbia, with all their attendant technologies and massive secondary effects . . . and a sharp rise in outlays for certain public and private services, which expanded disproportionately in rich countries (notably higher education, health services and travel)'.[3]

There is less agreement over the factors behind the downward phases, which are real structural crises. Some of the theories most frequently discussed are: a fall in the rate of profit, an increase in competition, an unmanageable contradiction between the rhythms of investment and consumption in an unplanned economy, the biological cycle of human beings (with a wave being equivalent to a generation) and, finally, revolutions, which, either as cause or effect, always take place in periods in which production is falling and unemployment is rising, and which add to the general disorganisation of the economy.

This potential for destabilisation explains why the ruling elite acknowledges the existence of these crises only when they are over, as past history that cannot interfere directly with the present. This was clearly the case in 1930:

'In the past, the Great Depression of the 1930s was not recognised as a downturn in the economic long wave. Rather, it was seen simply as a severe example of an ordinary business cycle downturn, accentuated by mistakes made by the Federal Reserve. By failing to see the true cause, governments and economists have missed an opportunity to learn from the past'.[4]

Table 4.1
The long-wave cycles

The cycles	The nature of the cycle	GDP growth (% per annum)	Causes and consequences
1762-1789	Recessionary		Beginning of industrial revolution disorganises production; shortage of Brazilian gold French Revolution/US independence
1792-1819	Expansionary		Consolidation of the industrial revolution and expansion of world markets
1819-1848	Recessionary	3.2	Increase in competition and decline in the rate of profit Communist Manifesto published/Popular Hungarian revolution
1848-1871	Expansionary	4.5	Expansion to new markets due to railway construction in five continents
1871-1895	Recessionary	1.2	Saturation of world markets and gold shortage; agrarian crisis Paris Commune
1895-1918	Expansionary	5.9	Formation of the monopolies; invention of car, electricity; expansion of markets
1918-1940	Recessionary	2.0	Overproduction; saturation of world market Russian Revolution/Fascism; World War II
1940-1967	Expansionary	5.2	Extension of new consumer habits; internationalisation of production and capital; average interest 4.75%; average unemployment 4.8%
1968-19??	Recessionary	2.5	Average unemployment 6.7%; average interest 9.5%; oil shock Iranian Revolution/debt crisis

Note: GDP figures are for Great Britain until 1913, and then for the USA.

Sources: Paul Craig and Kenneth E.F. Watt, *The Futurist*, April 1985; André Gunder Frank, *World Accumulation*, The Macmillan Press, 1978; Ernest Mandel, *Late Capitalism*, NLB, 1975.

The depression in the 1930s increased competition between the big corporations over markets, a dispute that was resolved by force in the Second World War. In the present crisis, characterised by chaotic fluctuations of the dollar, as the US has attempted to maintain artificially a hegemony no longer sustained by economic power, the capitalist centre has remained united and the tensions have been transferred to the periphery of the system, through a generalised crisis of indebtedness, punctuated by a few revolutions such as the Iranian and the Nicaraguan.

Latin America, which is a long way from the epicentre of the crises but is profoundly influenced by them, has been affected in paradoxical fashion by the shock waves. In the 1930s, as we saw in Chapter 1, the collapse in consumption in the United States ruined Latin America's export economy, based on farm products, and created a severe liquidity crisis. But, at the same time, because of this external stranglehold and the semi-paralysis that befell the big corporations, some Latin American economies, especially Argentina and Brazil, were able to take some steps forward in the industrialisation process.

This time, the shock wave has encountered a semi-industrialised, semi-urbanised Latin America, incorporated into US consumption patterns and with its industry integrated into both the world consumer goods market and the international financial market. The crisis has affected the continent in two phases. In the first, the fall in the rate of profit in the centre pushed monopoly capital towards Latin America and created, indirectly, favourable external conditions for the cycle of military regimes in the 1960s and 1970s. In the second phase, the crisis itself reached the periphery, in the form of both a decline in economic growth, the only source of legitimacy for the military regimes, and enormous foreign indebtedness, which, in its turn, weakened the dictatorships. The US crisis became a crisis for the Latin American dictatorships.

The emergence of the crisis

The crisis first emerged in the financial machinery of the system as a crisis in the hegemony of the dollar. When the Second World War ended, leaving Europe and Japan in ruins, only the dollar, because of its purchasing power in the US, had real value. Though it was formally victorious, Great Britain was left with most of its industry out of action, and the countries previously under its influence converted their sterling reserves into dollars. It was in this way that dollar supremacy was born, with the backing of American industry, responsible at that time for two-thirds of total output in the capitalist world.

Mindful of the 1930s depression and fearful of Soviet influence over the whole of eastern Europe, the US government decided to use its abundant reserves to fund a reconstruction programme for the very countries that it had helped to defeat. Under the Marshall Plan, about $13 billion was supplied for the reconstruction of Europe. Most of it went in the form of untied grants, to be spent as the countries wished. But, in practice, it was largely used to purchase US products — because there was virtually no alternative. (It was only later, after the European recovery, which meant that European countries began to compete with the US for markets, that the style of the aid changed. The money became tied to the purchase of US goods, a practice that was later copied by both the Japanese and the Europeans, as they competed for overseas customers. It became known as supplier's credit.[5])

With the Marshall Plan, the US sowed the seeds of its own downfall, though in the short term it was a great boon. It undertook the plan not because it was stupid, but because it was the only way of restoring demand, which had been decimated by the war. 'The contradictions of the US economy forced the United States to promote the recovery of Europe and Japan, even though it helped to erode their own comparative advantages', wrote the Brazilian economist, Monica Baer.[6]

In reality, behind its apparent strength, the US economy has, since the end of the Second World War, been grappling with dangerous internal tensions that are constantly threatening to push it into stagnation. This phenomenon, which is essential to the crisis that forced Latin America into excessive indebtedness, is often hidden or played down by conventional ideology. These tensions apparently spring from the high degree of capital concentration that characterises the US economy and from the virtual absence of moderating forces like the state companies in Europe. It is a pure form of capitalism in which crises are not restrained, but run wild. Capital is highly concentrated and, for this reason, it tends to over-accumulate and over-invest. So there tends to be a significant gap between the level of productive capacity installed by a corporation in anticipation of future demand, and the more modest level of real demand. As a result, idle capacity increases and the rate of profit falls. A significant part of the $10 billion invested annually by US corporations in the post-war period remained idle, which helps to explain the successive mini-recessions of 1954, 1958, 1961 and, finally, 1968, which marked the end of the rising phase of the cycle and the beginning of the decline.

Two mechanisms to combat the crisis

In an attempt to overcome this contradiction, the US economy developed two main mechanisms. The first was the armaments industry. Military expenditure is not a chance ingredient in the US economy, but its leading anti-recessionary mechanism. Estimates suggest that about one-quarter of US gross domestic product is generated, directly or indirectly, by military expenditure. Under the Reagan administration, this item has been consuming 34 per cent of the federal budget. This speeded-up militarisation, together with the administration's refusal to raise taxes, has created the ballooning public deficit that has pushed up interest rates and made a decisive contribution to the ruin of indebted countries in Latin America.[7]

Military expenditure has always been an economic necessity in American capitalism. As it does not interfere directly in the distribution of income nor in the market for civilian goods, it has also been politically convenient, the ideal anti-cyclical way of stimulating production. Like someone hooked on cocaine, the US economy became so dependent on military expenditure that, during the Reagan government, the need to increase this expenditure began to determine other policies. For the first time, the outlay on social welfare was sacrificed to the defence budget.

The second mechanism — and the one that made the biggest contribution first to the supremacy of the dollar and then to its collapse — was the transfer abroad of US factories. Thanks to the continental size of the United States, its companies grew, safe from international conflicts, and, when they had covered all the domestic market, they naturally believed themselves to be equipped to dominate the rest of the planet, almost as if it were a natural extension of their home market. Taking advantage of the monopoly of the dollar as the international currency in the post-war world, they bought and built factories throughout the world, particularly in Europe, where the reconstruction programmes and the economic gains of the working class had led to very rapid growth in the consumption of durable goods.

Table 4.2

The dollar empire: the expansion of American capitalism in the world

	1914	1938	1968	1978
Item				
All countries' foreign investments ($ bn)	14.3	26.4	108.0	386.0
US foreign investments ($ bn)	2.6	7.3	65.0	162.0
US/total (%)	18.5	27.7	55.0	43.0
Foreign investments in Latin America as % of total	32.7	30.8	17.0	14.5
US investments in Latin America as % of US total investments	1.6	4.1	19.8	15.0
No. of subsidiaries of US transnationals	122	1,763	23,282	33,000
No. of subsidiaries of US transnationals in Latin America	n.a	315	5,436	n.a.

Sources: Geraldo Muller, *Economia Mundial Contemporanea*, Cadernos Cebrap, no. 7; UNO report, 1970; Aristoteles Moura, *Capitais Estrangeiros no Brasil*, Brasiliense, 1960; *Estudos Economicos para a America Latina*, UNO, 1970.

At the end of the 1960s, at the peak of the cycle of expansion, US multinationals accounted for well over half of all foreign investment in capitalist countries (*see* Table 4.2), with an annual turnover of about $60 billion and profits of about $8 billion.[8] The companies' preference for Europe had led to a fall in Latin America's share of total US foreign investment from 31 per cent in 1950 to only 20 per cent in 1968. Even so, whole sectors of Latin American industry fell under the control of transnationals, headed by American companies, particularly in Mexico, Brazil, Argentina and Venezuela. These countries, which were to become the most indebted, accounted for 85 per cent of US investment south of the Rio Grande.[9]

Wielding more resources than those handled by many governments, and taking advantage of legal loopholes, transnationals both created tax havens and built up the eurodollar market as ways of completely internationalising dollar transactions and avoiding the controls of interfering governments. The eurodollar market, in particular, was to be of enormous importance to Latin America and is discussed in detail later (*see* Chapter 6). Thus the regulatory power of central banks was reduced, and speculative flows of money brought chaos to the monetary system set up at Bretton Woods.

The same degree of concentration came to dominate production. As the transnationals scattered their factories throughout the world, optimising factors of production on a global scale, so the relative weight of manufactured exports shipped from the US fell significantly (from one-fifth of the total from capitalist countries in 1950 to one-seventh in 1970). The world became a single chess-board, as integration intensified and economies became ever more deeply enmeshed. Economies such as Latin America, situated on the periphery, became increasingly dependent on economic developments completely outside their control. The economy became global, and so too did its recessions.

Two fuels, available on a practically unlimited scale and thus at cheap prices, played a crucial role in this cycle: oil, which fed the machines that provided transport in the economy; and grain, which fed the people. The British historian, E.J. Hobsbawm, believes that cheap oil was probably the single most important cause of the post-war boom. Throughout this period oil never cost more than two cents a litre — less than mineral water. World oil consumption increased spectacularly to 10 million barrels a day. In the view of the US economist W.W. Rostow, the availability of cheap grain was crucial in keeping down inflation in the US. And inflation was considered the best single indicator of a country's economic health.[10]

Thanks to extremely cheap energy, US patterns of consumption and production spread to extremely poor societies, such as Latin America, which by ordinary rules of common sense should have had other priorities. Health, education and urban mass transport were relegated to second place with the arrival of the transnationals' car assembly plants, which reinforced local elitism and created new dependencies on oil and imported electrical goods.

At the end of 25 years of this euphoric expansion, the aggregate gross domestic product of all the capitalist economies had grown three and a half times. World trade, boosted by the close trading links between transnationals and their subsidiaries, had grown fourfold, reaching $200 billion a year. It was the cycle of fastest growth in the history of the capitalist economies. Capitalism seemed immortal and, from the late 1950s, competed with communism even for control of outer space. Freed from the '1929 syndrome', renowned economists discussed the new mechanisms that had made it possible for capitalism to escape from its cyclical crises.

The re-emergence of the crisis

But the cyclical crisis returned that summer (1968), slowly, as if no more than a moderate recession to add to the four experienced since the war. In the following year, US growth fell half a point and the recovery, in addition to being short-lived, didn't come until 30 months later, compared with an average of 19 months in the four previous recessions. President Richard Nixon, who had come to office in 1969 with tough fiscal policies, belatedly increased public spending in 1971. But the move came too late, and, in any case, proved ineffective.

The crisis led to a sizeable and irreversible decline in all the main indicators of the US economy: an increase in grain prices and in inflation (*see* Table 4.3); a fall in industrial productivity and a consequent decline in the rate of profit; and the loss of foreign markets to competitors that it had helped to reconstruct — Japan and West Germany. Entire sectors of industry became obsolete, with the progressive erosion of the technological foundation of the US pattern of consumption. The relative weight of the US gross domestic product fell from about half of the world total just after the war to a little over one-third. In contrast, Japan's share jumped from an insignificant amount to 8 per cent, taking markets away first from Great Britain and then from the United States. After exhausting the cheap oil reserves in Texas, the US ceased to be a net exporter and became a net importer.

Table 4.3
The numbers of the US crisis

	1960	1965	1968	1970	1974
Unemployment becomes chronic (% of labour force unemployed)	5.5	4.5	3.6	4.9	5.6
Inflation increases (change in consumer price index)	1.6	1.7	4.2	5.9	11.0
Current account goes into the red ($ bn)	1.8	4.3	−0.9	−0.3	−5.0
Foreign debt swells ($ bn)	34.0	70.0	75.0	84.4	150.0
Gold reserves fall ($ bn)	21.8	17.8	12.0	11.8	11.6

Note: The US foreign debt includes all liabilities, except foreign investment in the US. The gold reserves include an additional $1bn in 1972, and another $1.4bn in 1973, as a result of exclusively accounting increases stemming from the higher dollar price of gold (dollar devaluations).

Source: *The Economic Report of the President*, February 1975.

Unlike its response in 1930, US industry reacted to the crisis by increasing its involvement in the periphery of the global economy, especially in Latin America, where higher rates of profit were to be obtained. In this first phase, from 1968 to the first oil shock, there was enormous capital liquidity on the world financial market. 'For the first time ever, the influx of capital is greater than the outflow through interest and profits', stated the Economic Commission for Latin America's annual report,[11] optimistically. Investment in basic industries in Latin America, which had been limping along at 2 per cent a year, jumped to 13 per cent in 1968 and remained at between 9 and 12 per cent in the following four years. US growth fell to just half its earlier level, confirming once again the long wave theory.

The outside world began to become aware of the US crisis when the country's trade surplus, which had been running at around $4−5 billion, dropped to next to nothing in 1968. The trade surplus was one of just two ways in which the US recovered the dollars it invested abroad in the purchase of companies and land. The other mechanism was the inflow from royalties and dividends (which brought in about $4 billion). All other US transactions resulted in a net outflow: military expenditure, pensions, government expenditure and aid to repressive governments consumed about $12 billion a year; and investments by subsidiaries of US companies used up another $3 billion.

The disappearance of the trade surpluses destabilised the dollar, revealing what some people had suspected for some time: that the dollar did not have the required backing in gold. Under the Bretton Woods agreement, that created the post-war monetary system, each dollar was automatically convertible into a fixed quantity of gold (0.888 grammes). But, when those holding dollars looked more carefully at the US national accounts, they were alarmed to discover that the US Treasury only had 13,500 tonnes of gold, equivalent to $12 billion, or less than one-sixth of the $75 billion held by foreigners.[12]

Astute creditors had been demanding repayment in the form of gold for some time, with about $1 billion being converted each year. The French central bank had been particularly active, taking a large volume of gold from the US Treasury. In July 1971, US reserves fell to their lowest level since the Great Depression: $13.5 billion, of which only $10 billion was in gold. The US foreign debt was already $109.6 billion, of which $45 billion was owed to other countries' central banks.

The end of the gold standard

The fragility of the dollar unleashed violent and repeated capital flows with each announcement of a new US deficit. On 15 August 1971, after a week of the most violent oscillations ever on the financial markets, President Nixon decreed, unilaterally, the end of the convertibility of dollars into gold. This meant, inevitably, the end of the gold standard — the fixed parity between the dollar and gold, and between the dollar and other currencies. The US Treasury would no longer guarantee in gold the value of the dollar. As a result of the unilateral decision of the US government, the monetary order set up by international agreement at Bretton Woods collapsed overnight. It was the first of a series of spectacular manoeuvres by which the US managed to slough off its international responsibilities and to postpone its crisis for more than 15 years.

With the collapse in the gold standard, the US dollar lost about 7 per cent of its value with respect to the other leading currencies. All those, including Latin American central banks, who had trusted in the Bretton Woods agreement and kept their reserves in dollars were dealt a double blow — they lost for ever 7 per cent of their reserves, and they said goodbye to their right to convert automatically their reserves into gold.

The US economy should have been suffering from a serious exchange crisis for some time. That this had not happened was due to a curious mechanism arising from the hegemony of the dollar. The only country in which the dollar was the national currency, yielding interest in ordinary financial investments, was the US. The same dollars that were invested abroad by the Americans in the purchase of companies, in aid to repressive regimes and in wars, came back to the country to be invested in treasury bonds, to be used to purchase property, or to be lent to big corporations. It was a magical circle, a near-perfect system which, in theory, could go on for ever, like a perpetual motion machine.

But with the growing US deficits, the dollars that went back to the US did not belong to Americans, but to foreigners — central banks, big companies and individuals. As a result of world expansion, not through the conquest of territory, but through money, the US became heavily indebted. The US foreign debt had doubled in ten years, and it seemed that it would double again in even less time

— such exponential growth did indeed happen; it lay behind the violent increase in interest rates that ruined Latin America in 1981.

The devaluation of the dollar reduced the principal of this debt by 7 per cent. But the crisis was not resolved. In December 1971, the governments of the ten richest capitalist countries (the US, the EEC, Japan, Sweden and Canada) met at the Smithsonian Institute in Washington and tried in vain to patch over the cracks in the monetary system. They backed the devaluation, increasing the official price of gold in the central banks' reserves from $35 an ounce (31.1035 grammes) to $38, equivalent to a 7.89 per cent devluation. They tried to restrict exchange fluctuations to no more than 2.25 per cent of the new parities — double the margin established at Bretton Woods. But they did not reinstate the convertibility of the dollar, and it continued to fluctuate wildly.

The monetary chaos reached a climax in February 1973, with the announcement of a US trade deficit of $6.5 billion in 1972. The foreign debt had risen to $110 billion. So the US government swindled its creditors yet again, forcing through a new devaluation of the dollar. But the large-scale selling of the dollar continued. The central banks, which had the largest dollar reserves, tried to stop the dollar slide by buying yet more dollars — several billion in a single day. Finally all exchange operations were closed for nine days at the beginning of August 1973.

Since the beginning of the crisis, the dollar had lost 23 per cent of its exchange value. It was the beginning of the current crisis in American capitalism. The US had already begun to transfer most of the cost outside the country, establishing a pattern that was to become ever more pronounced in subsequent years. As we shall see, the burden was to be borne firstly by US creditors and then, increasingly, by debtor nations, particularly in Latin America.

Notes

1. 'All systems stop', *The Economist*, 30 November 1974, p. 85.
2. Two economists, Nicolai Kondratieff and Joseph Schumpeter, studied long waves. The most recent analysis is J.J. van Dujin, *The Long Wave in Economic Life*.
3. W.W. Rostow, *The Barbaric Counter Revolution*, University of Texas Press, 1983; and see 'Caught by Kondratieff', *New York Times*, 8 March 1977.
4. Jay W. Forrester, *The Futurist*, June 1985.
5. See Cheryl Payer, *The Debt Trap*, Pelican Books, 1974.
6. Monica Baer, 'A Natureza Financeira da Crise e Suas Perspectivas', PNPE, mimeographed, 1984.
7. The average annual military expenditure, as a percentage of GDP, was: 1939−40: 2%; 1941: 11%; 1942−45: 40%; 1946−50: 6%; 1951−57: 13.4%; 1958−68: 10.7%; 1969−74: 6.6%; 1974−85: 5.2%. Source: *The Economic Report of the President*, 1985.
8. UNO, Report on Multinational Companies, 1971.
9. UNO, Economic Report for Latin America, 1970.
10. E.J. Hobsbawm, *The Crisis and the Outlook*, London 1975; W.W. Rostow, op.cit.
11. UNO, Economic Report for Latin America, 1972.
12. See *The Economic Report of the President*, 1975.

5. The Dictators of the Debt

The sad tale of the alliance between Latin American oligarchies and foreign capital

Hicieron una línea negra:
'Aquí nosotros, porfiristas
de México, "caballeros"
de Chile, pitucos
del Jockey Club de Buenos Aires,
engomados filibusteros
del Uruguay, pisaverdes
ecuatorianos, clericales
señoritos de todas partes.'

'Allí vosotros, rotos, cholos,
pelados de México, gauchos,
amontonados en pocilgas;
desamparados, andrajosos,
piojentos, pililos, canalla,
desbaratados, miserables,
sucios, perezosos, pueblo.'

Pablo Neruda, *Canto General*[1]

International bankers were perfectly willing by their loans to maintain dictators in power and to be party to the suppression of every natural right of citizens of South American republics. Indeed, they contributed the money, in some instances, for the destruction of liberty itself . . . loans were made sometimes to maintain dictators in power, dictators who laughed to scorn every fundamental principle of liberty.

Hiram Johnson, US Republican Senator, in a speech in the 1930s

Latin America is much better known for its dictators — the accumulators of the debt — than for its mass-based struggle against repression. And yet Latin Americans have a notable revolutionary tradition. One of the most remarkable revolutions is the Mexican, the first in this century, which left behind it half a million dead, and inspired liberation movements in almost every Spanish-speaking Latin American country. Another extraordinary event was the 14,000-mile Long March undertaken in Brazil by the rebel Prestes column in the 1920s, before Mao Zedong's much more famous Long March in China.

This revolutionary tradition, which erupts from time to time like lava from a volcano, can be seen as a reaction to the extremely conservative nature of the forces that dominate the continent: the local oligarchies, descendants of the Spanish and Portuguese *conquistadores*, who set up a mercantile economy that greatly concentrated wealth; and foreign capital, particularly US, that has played a predatory role south of the Rio Grande.

Though it can be paternalist and populist during its benign phases, this coalition becomes dictatorial and cruel when threatened by mass-based organisations. With a few partial exceptions, such as the Bolivian revolution in 1952, the US government has been consistent in its efforts to defeat all endeavours to change the essential status quo in Latin America. During the Second World War, the US supported some progressive forces in Latin America as part of a general alignment against neo-fascism, financing a few economic development projects as part of the war effort. But, as soon as the war ended, it returned to its old predatory policies, in both the political and the economic camps.

The doctrine of 'collective security'

The Cold War became a pretext for suppressing popular movements. In 1947, the US Secretary of State, John Foster Dulles, used it to win Latin American governments over to the concept of 'collective security', a diabolic doctrine which has been used time and again by reactionary governments to crush mass-based movements on the rare occasions that they have become sufficiently well-organised to set their sights on power. It was with reference to this doctrine that the Treaty of Reciprocal Military Assistance was created in Rio de Janeiro in 1947. And it is this treaty that is always invoked by the US State Department to justify intervention when mass-based struggles have reached a critical point in a country in the region. The US has long known that the best way of preventing revolution in the region is to select the best organised of the popular movements and to squash them, thus stopping them from encouraging other movements in other countries by their example.

The Marshall Plan was greeted with considerable excitement by Latin American intellectuals, who during the war had become aware of the inadequacies of the basic infrastructure in the continent. The Brazilians had even drawn up a plan, entitled SALTE (Health, Food, Transport, Energy) to eliminate the worst bottlenecks, with an outlay of only $100 million.[2] But it soon became clear that the US would be making unilateral transfers only to Europe, not to Latin America.

In the two decades following the Second World War, the World Bank and the Inter-American Development Bank together lent just $4 billion to the whole of Latin America.[3] They were long-term loans, at fixed interest rates, intended to promote the modernisation of the region and to introduce the concept of economic planning. These loans undoubtedly made a contribution, but many of their benefits were undermined by the tendency both to link them to the purchase of equipment from the industrialised countries and to use them to support investments by the transnational companies. So the idea of national economic growth became merged with — and even subordinated to — the expansion plans of specific economic groups. To qualify for loans from the international financial organisations, Latin American countries also had to reiterate their commitment to the American idea of free enterprise and open their economies completely to foreign capital. This was not necessarily in their long-term interest.

Even during this period, when about two-thirds of the capital flowing into Latin America came from governments (*see* Table 5.1), Latin America was in fact sending out of the continent more money in interest payments and dividends than it was receiving in loans and investment. The figures come from the Economic

Table 5.1
From risk capital to financial capital

Flows of different types of capital to the developing world
(% share going to each type)

	1959-67	1968-69	1970-72	1973-78	1979-81	1982
Official loans	66.7	57.8	53.3	46.3	48.9	52.7
Private capital:	33.3	42.2	46.7	53.7	51.1	47.3
direct investment	0.0	20.5	17.7	14.7	13.9	12.1
commercial loans	25.4	8.1	19.2	28.5	25.7	25.3
suppliers' credit	7.9	13.6	9.8	10.5	11.5	9.9

Source: Monica Baer, A Natureza Financeira da Crise e Suas Perspectivas, PNPE, mimeographed, 1984

Commission for Latin America (ECLA), which was the region's first independent centre of regional economic studies, set up by the Argentinian economist Raúl Prebisch, under the auspices of the United Nations.

ECLA studies show that, during the 19 years from 1950 to the end of the post-war boom (1969), Latin America sent abroad in foreign remittances $28.4 billion, while $20.1 billion came in as investment and loans (*see* Table 5.2). The loss of $8 billion is equivalent to an annual outflow of almost half a billion dollars.[4]

It was evident that Latin America's growing integration in the world financial market was beginning to drain resources out of the region, rather than bringing money in to fund development. It was a point that was not lost on Latin American economists. Writing at that time, the Brazilian economist Celso Furtado warned: 'Unless the financial institutions become much more active, the region will soon not only be remitting abroad more profits than it receives in investments but also be contracting loans just to service old debts.'[5] A similar warning was made by the Pearson Commission, from the World Bank, which pointed out that interest payments and repayments of principal had consumed 87 per cent of the loans contracted during 1965 and 1966.

To avert a balance of payments crisis, Latin America needed an injection of money from abroad, just as a patient suffering from leukaemia needs blood transfusions. From 1970 to 1973, Latin America borrowed $23.4 billion, more than the accumulated total for the previous 20 years. This duly staved off the crisis, but only at the price of sowing the seeds of a much more serious balance of payments crisis in the future.

Local economists, most of them linked to ECLA, began to use these statistics to explain the mysterious exchange crises that periodically assailed the region, elaborating the theory of dependency. The structuralist school was born, with its reformist ideas for ending Latin American stagnation by redistributing wealth and increasing the role of the state. The mechanisms by which a small initial influx of foreign capital could be used to justify in subsequent years growing remittances of interest and profits began to be uncovered (*see* box, p. 50).

The US government tried to close down ECLA as early as 1951 because of the repercussions of its theories and studies, which were being carried out beyond the control of the ideological centres of the industrialised countries. But the US pressure failed, largely because of the resistance of President Getulio Vargas, in

Table 5.2
The bleeding of Latin America, 1950-73
(net capital flows, $m)

	Inflow	Outflow	Balance	Accumulated Balance
1950−59	7,501.9	−10,281.4	−2,779.5	−2,779.5
1960−69	12,614.2	−18,072.2	−5,458.0	−8,237.5
Total	20,116.1	−28,353.6	−8,237.5	−8,237.5

And the injection of finance that led to the snowballing of the debt:

				Final balance
1970-73	23,400	-13,100	10,300	2,062.5

Note: Some services, such as royalties, which should be part of the capital outflow, are not included in the figures.

Sources: *Estudos Economicos para a America Latina*, UNO, 1970, p.46, for 1950-69 period; and *Cuadernos Cepal* no. 49, for 1970-73 period.

Brazil. (With the wave of military coups at the end of the 1960s, ECLA's studies lost some of their bite, but the current crisis, which has coincided with the return to civilian government in Brazil, Argentina, Uruguay and Bolivia, has restored part of their old vigour.)

With the larger influx of foreign capital, the World Bank and the International Monetary Fund began to lose their importance. Transnational companies began to finance themselves with private capital, in the form of equity investments, suppliers' credit and loans from the euromarket (*see* Table 5.1). Official loans, accounting for almost 70 per cent of the total capital inflow into Latin America until the end of the 1960s, fell to half of the total after the eruption of the US crisis in the early 1970s.

Rather than alarming the local bourgeoisie, whether industrial or agrarian, the mushrooming foreign debt reassured them, cementing their alliance with international capital. For the growing dependence on exports meant that the local governments had to maintain both export incentives and devalued exchange rates. While boosting export earnings, these also meant that the exporters obtained large amounts of local currency for their dollars and were able to retain their privileges, while the economic and political demands of the mass of workers were duly repressed. It was largely for this reason that even the industrialisation in the 1960s and 1970s, which greatly developed domestic markets in the region, also established as one of its objectives the increase of exports.

Opposition is suppressed

All attempts to change this state of affairs were repressed with decisive support from the State Department in the US. After attempting to carry out a broad programme of agrarian reform that included unproductive lands owned by the United Fruit Company, Jacobo Arbenz, the President of Guatemala, was overthrown in 1954 by a mercenary army organised by the CIA. It was in this way that began, in the key country in Central America, one of the longest and bloodiest dictator-

The miracle of the multiplication of profit

According to figures from the US Department of Trade, the average annual return on US capital invested in Latin America in 1978 was 16 per cent. Let us see what this means in practice. Let us take a company investing $100 million in a Latin American country. Let us suppose that, out of the $16 million profit that it gains from this investment in the first year, it sends home $10 million and reinvests locally $6m. This pattern is then repeated for the next seven years. Let us see what this means.

($ m)

	Profit	Annual Remittance	Reinvestment	Registered Capital	Accumulated Remittance
Year 1	16	10	6	100	10
Year 2	17	10	7	106	20
Year 3	19	12	7	113	32
Year 4	21	13	8	120	45
Year 5	22	14	8	128	59
Year 6	23	15	8	136	74
Year 7	25	15	10	144	89
Year 8	26	16	10	154	105
Total	**169**	**105**	**64**	**164**	**105**

In just eight years, the mother company has recovered its initial investment of $100 million, and the capital invested in the Latin American country has increased to $164 million. It is in this way that US investments in Latin America were able to grow from $10 billion in 1966 to $32 billion in 1978, with only a small part of this money being effectively sent from the US to Latin America.

ships ever known in the continent, responsible for the deaths of thousands of peasants. In the same year, in Brazil, President Vargas was driven to suicide by a campaign undertaken jointly by the export sector and pro-American military groups who were opposed to the government's policies of populism and nationalism.

Vargas had nationalised the oil industry, fixed an annual ceiling on profit remittances of 10 per cent of registered capital, and had limited annual interest payments to 8 per cent of the principal. Examining the foreign capital register, he discovered that, from the end of the war to 1952, Brazil had been a net exporter of capital, sending more money abroad in payments of interest, royalties and dividends than it had received in direct investment and loans. Comparing Brazilian and US trade figures, he also uncovered under-billing and over-billing frauds, worth $150 million in just an 18 month period. Another remarkable discovery was that in a period (1940−43) during which Brazil was actually a net exporter of capital, US investments had managed to increase by $770 million. 'Foreign company profits even reached 500 per cent a year. In the declarations of imported goods there are repeated frauds worth over $100 million a year . . .',[6] wrote Vargas in his farewell letter. The accusations were very similar to the ones that President Salvador Allende, in Chile, was to make almost 20 years later.

After the death of Vargas, Resolution 113 was introduced, considered even today as the key document that gave foreign companies control over large sectors of Brazilian industry. It allowed foreigners to import all kinds of machinery, even second-hand ones, without paying tax and using central bank dollars. These imports could be registered as capital investment, thus increasing even further the level of future profit remittances.

With the US economy in recession, the head companies of transnationals transferred whole production lines of obsolete equipment to Brazil, using dollars supplied to their subsidiaries by the central bank and registering these transfers as capital inflows. ('Satraps, sold a thousand times'[7] was how Pablo Neruda described the Latin Americans who colluded in this rape of the continent.)

In 1955 there arose in Latin America the first grandiose version of the alliance between the local oligarchy and foreign capital, creating a model that would would be copied in different versions throughout the world, including in Iran under the Shah. In Brazil in 1955, President Juscelino Kubitschek, in the midst of a serious exchange crisis caused by the collapse in the price of coffee and under growing popular pressure, resisted IMF pressure to adopt a conventional austerity programme. Instead, he launched an ambitious programme for 'Fifty years of development in five', attracting transnationals with generous tax incentives and with infrastructure support.

For the first time since the war, Brazil received a net capital influx for some years. Even so, only $149 million came in during the five-year period (1956−60), less than half the amount that Brazil lost with the fall in coffee prices. With this money, almost all of the new industry was owned by transnationals or associated with them.

The first defeat for the US

Fidel Castro's victory in Cuba in 1959, which installed the first socialist economy in the continent, alerted the US to the risks of its predatory policies. The Pentagon extended to the continent its 'domino' theory, according to which the 'fall' of one country to communism would inevitably lead to the loss of others. The Bay of Pigs invasion was quickly organised. It was the United States' first significant defeat in the continent.

The Alliance for Progress — the Latin American version of the Marshall Plan — was drawn up as a result of this disaster. Investment in social welfare programmes was fixed at $10 billion. But sabotage by local oligarchies, who were opposed to modernisation, and the procrastinations of the US Congress reduced the disbursements. Very little was achieved, even in Colombia, which was selected to become the showcase of free enterprise.

At the same time, a powerful repressive machine was assembled to avoid new 'Cubas'. Washington became more determined than ever to support strong regimes as the best barrier against communism. So, once again, the spectre of communism was used to reinforce repression, paving the way indirectly for the cycle of dictatorships in the 1960s and for the swelling of the foreign debt.

A wide-ranging system of military indoctrination was set up, with its base in the US Army's School of the Americas in Panama. In just two years (1962−63), new doctrines about the 'internal enemy' and new methods of counter-insurgency were instilled into 600 officers from many different Latin American countries. Over 60,000 officers had been trained in this school by 1976, which gives an average of 2,320 a year. This means that two out of three senior Latin American officers were trained at this centre. Its role in the establishment of military dictatorships in later years is evident. 'I cannot exaggerate the importance of having in positions of leadership (in Latin America) men that have direct experience of how the Americans think and act', said Defense Secretary Robert McNamara.[8]

In 1962, President John Kennedy set up a new agency — the Office of Public Safety — which trained and sent back to the Third World 400 specialists in repression. When it was dissolved in 1975, this agency had trained 7,500 policemen and supplied $200 million-worth of arms to Third World countries. Among other achievements, it had set up the '*casco blanco*' anti-riot squad in the Dominican Republic, created a war unit in Caracas and organised the Institute of Criminology and Identification in Brasilia.[9]

The succession of military coups

The series of military coups began soon after this. The Argentine president, Arturo Frondizi, was deposed as early as 1962, being followed by the decisive overthrow of President João Goulart in Brazil in 1964. John Foster Dulles once predicted that wherever Brazil went, the rest of Latin America would follow. And on this occasion at least he was right. Ten years after the Brazilian coup almost the entire continent was under military control.

The important military coup in Brazil was organised by the main leaders of the national bourgeoisie, who had prepared in advance a programme for opening up the economy to foreign capital and dismantling mass-based movements.[10] As there was virtually no resistance to the coup, this programme was carried out easily, serving later as a model for General Augusto Pinochet in Chile and the civilian ally of the military, Juan María Bordaberry, in Uruguay.

But in Chile, there first took place an important reformist endeavour that was democratic and peaceful, through the election of President Salvador Allende in 1970, leading a coalition of mass-based parties. Chile was then the foremost world exporter of copper and had one of the largest foreign debts in Latin America: $3 billion for a gross domestic product of $8 billion and a population of 10 million. Over the previous 50 years, transnational companies had invested only $1 billion in Chile but had remitted seven times this amount ($7.2 billion), with Anaconda and Kennecott, the two US companies that controlled the copper sector, accounting for over half ($4.2 billion) of this.[11]

Allende was overthrown in 1973 by a coup organised once again by the CIA, aided by the transnationals headed by ITT, together with local oligarchies (*see* box p. 54). Chile's foreign debt, which stands today at around $35 billion, is the joint responsibility of General Pinochet, who came to power with the coup, of the transnationals and local businessmen who helped him, and of the US State Department which encouraged him. One can argue over the exact allocation of responsibility between these protagonists. But what is evident is that it is not the Chilean people who are responsible. This argument, so clear in the case of Chile, can be applied, to a greater or lesser degree, to the other countries of Latin America. The Chilean case helps explain why Latin America's rulers let themselves be deceived so easily. For, in fact, they were not taken in: they were accomplices — apart from a few, who were overthrown.

The Nicaraguan revolution

With the victory of the Sandinistas in Nicaragua in 1979 and the election of President Ronald Reagan in 1980 in the wake of a profound conservative revival in the US — the result of its serious economic crisis — US strategy became more sophisticated. On the one hand, the government decided to topple the Sandinistas through indirect military intervention by arming the contras and applying low intensity warfare, waged at all levels of society. On the other hand, it encouraged the careful replacement of the dictatorships it had helped to install after the Cuban revolution, putting in their place more democratic governments.

This two-pronged approach had two objectives: to isolate further Nicaragua, which was not a formal bourgeois democracy; and to legitimise Latin America's foreign debts, before mass-based movements not only overthrew the dictatorial governments, but also repudiated the debts that they had contracted.

The US government has always tried to justify its opposition to left-of-centre, mass-based movements by referring to the 'communist threat'. 'There can be no negotiated solution either with the Sandinists or with the FMLN guerrillas in El Salvador, just as it would have been impossible to persuade Lenin to give up the totalitarianism of the Bolsheviks. . . The only answer is to overthrow them', said Fred Ikle, Under-Secretary for Defense in the US government.[12]

Because of the force of the US anti-communist rhetoric, many observers criticise US policy in Latin America for being a 'mere by-product' of the Cold War. But the truth seems far more prosaic. Recent analyses of US policy suggest that the State Department operates in the defence of the specific interests of US companies and banks. Almost invariably the political strategy adopted has been to support local conservative elites in return for support from them. US strategy is 'to reinforce privileged elites, in return for protection for American investments', writes Richard McCall, a specialist in foreign relations in the US Democratic Party.[13]

Latin America today is thus living in a paradoxical situation. The bulk of the

A chronology of military coups in the early days of the debt crisis

1962—USA
The American government creates a counter-insurgency programme, training over 60,000 officers from all over Latin America during the next 15 years. It sets up a public security agency, which sends 400 specialists in police repression to Third World countries.

1962—Argentina
The military overthrows president Arturo Frondizi, beginning a cycle of coups that lasts until 1984, when the Falklands/Malvinas defeat ends the dictatorship. About 30,000 opponents of the regime 'disappear' under military rule. The foreign debt reaches $48 billion.

1963—Ecuador
Military coup overthrows President Julio Arosemena.

1963—Dominican Republic
Military overthrows Juan Bosch, the first elected president after 31 years of dictatorship under the US ally, Leonidas Trujillo. Two years later, the US Marines invade the country with the support of six Latin American countries to squash the popular insurrection led by Francisco Caamano to bring Bosch back to power.

1964—Brazil
With US support, the military overthrows President João Goûlart, beginning 21 years of military rule. The foreign debt leaps from $2.9 billion in 1964 to $103 billion in 1984. Almost 5,000 opponents are imprisoned, killed or forced into exile.

1965—Bolivia
General Rene Barrientos overthrows President Victor Paz Estenssoro, starting the 'long night' that, with a brief interval in 1970—71, lasts until 1978. US support for the coup is rewarded by opening up the country to transnationals. The foreign debt reaches $3 billion.

1968—Peru
The military overthrows President Belaúnde Terry, who is carrying out social reforms. Later, the military regime itself takes on a nationalist character.

1973—Chile
The military, supported by the CIA, overthrows President Salvador Allende, who two years earlier had denounced the financial exploitation of the country by transnationals. General Augusto Pinochet sets up one of the longest-lasting military dictatorships in the continent. The foreign debt increases from $3.6 billion to $14 billion.

1973—Uruguay
After defeating the Tupamaros urban guerrillas, the military carries out a coup, setting up a military regime that is to last until 1984. The debt, which was $300 million in 1973, reaches $3 billion.

With the coup in Uruguay, the cycle is completed. All of the Southern Cone of Latin America, including Paraguay, which has been ruled by General Alfredo Stroessner since 1954, is under military control.

foreign debt was contracted by dictators, whom most Latin Americans never supported, but who for many years were backed by companies, banks and governments in the creditor nations, particularly the US. The Latin American countries have for the most part thrown off these dictatorships, but, partly as the result of US pressure and partly owing to the setbacks experienced by the mass-based movements through the long years of military rule, they have not taken the next step. The Latin American people have not seriously challenged either the power of the conservative elites that supported the dictatorships or the legitimacy of the debts contracted by the dictators. The debt's dictators have gone, but not yet the dictatorship of the debt.

Notes

1. Pablo Neruda, from 'Los Oligarquias' in *Canto General*. The extract is virtually untranslatable; it begins 'They made a black line:/"Here's us . . .' followed by a string of expressions meaning 'the rich' in the slang of different Latin American countries, continuing, in the second part, ' "There's you . . .', followed by a corresponding collection of terms for 'the poor'.

2. Celso Furtado, *A Fantasia Organisada*, Paz e Terra, 1986.

3. Ibid.

4. Estudos Econômicos para a América Latina, 1970, and *Cuadernos de la Cepal*, no. 49.

5. Celso Furtado, *The Economic Development of Latin America*, Cambridge University Press, 1970.

6. Aristoteles Moura, *Capitais Estrangeiros no Brasil*, Brasiliense, 1960; Cibilis da Rocha Viana, *Estratregia do Desenvolvimento Brasileiro*, Civ, Brasileira, 1967; and Pinto Ferreira, *Capitais Estrangeiros e Dívida Externa do Brasil*, Brasiliense, 1965.

7. Pablo Neruda, *Canto General*.

8. *The US Military Apparatus*, NACLA report, 1970.

9. See Michael T. Klare, *Supplying Repression*, Institute for Policy Studies, Washington, 1977; and *The US Military Apparatus*, NACLA report, 1970.

10. René Dreifuss, *1964 — A Conquista do Estado*, Vozes, São Paulo, 1981.

11. Dale Johnson, *The Chilean Road to Socialism*, 1973.

12. Richard Newfarmer, (ed), *From Gunboats to Diplomacy*, The Johns Hopkins University Press, 1984.

13. Ibid.

6. The Trap of the Floating Interest Rate

The remarkable story of the euromarket, which is not monitored by any central bank, and does not have fixed interest rates nor reserve funds for emergencies

> . . . *organized* capital may very well make the discovery that the interest rate can be maintained above the level of free competition, if the resulting surplus can be sent abroad . . . Now it is true that capital is nowhere cartelized. But it is everywhere subject to the guidance of the big banks . . .
>
> **J.A. Schumpeter**, trans. Heinz Norden, *Imperialism and Social Classes* (Basil Blackwell, Oxford, 1951) p. 106

> More and more, bankers dealing in the Eurocurrency market are breaking one of banking's sacred rules: we are lending long and borrowing short. True, perhaps, banks are protecting the rate by a floating rate. Still and all, we are making seven-year loans and financing ourselves usually on a 90- to 180-day basis. . . . a sudden change in conditions (and political situations often change rapidly and unexpectedly) could create a measure of illiquidity in the Eurocurrency market.
>
> **Frederick Heldring**, vice-chairman, Philadelphia National Bank, quoted in *Euromoney*, March 1973

Though it involves the whole Third World, the debt crisis is essentially a Latin American tragedy. The Peruvian economist and former finance minister, Pedro Pablo Kuczinsky, showed that in 1982 Latin America owed half of the Third World's debt and that to pay off just the \$300-billion principal of this debt it would need to use all its export earnings for three years and five months. The rest of the Third World, he added, could pay off its debt with the earnings of just one year and one month.[1]

A mechanism for extracting income

Latin America's debt has become so large that it can never be repaid. As a result, it no longer belongs in the ordinary business world. Instead it has become both a mechanism for permanently extracting income for the private banks and also as an instrument of domination. Whereas in other regions of the Third World, the payment of interest accounts for, at most, 2 per cent of the gross domestic product, in Latin America the main debtors have been spending between 5 and 8 per cent (*see* Table 6.1). Whereas in indebted countries in Asia and Africa about 15−25 per cent of export earnings is spent on debt servicing (interest plus principal repayments), the proportion has been more than half of export earnings in Mexico, Ecuador, Peru and Chile, 87 per cent in Brazil and a remarkable 100 per cent in Argentina.[2] As we saw in Chapter 1, this has forced each country to cut back severely on imports.

Why has Latin America been forced to spend so much on interest payments?

The single most important factor has been the region's heavy dependence on floating interest rates. While only a third of the debts of Asian and African countries (with the exception of Nigeria) are charged at floating interest rates, the proportion is 70 per cent in Latin America (reaching 88 per cent in Venezuela). With the surge in market rates in the late 1970s, interest payments absorbed an ever larger proportion of export earnings, forcing the countries to get deeper and deeper into debt and turning the debt into a snowball. The *coup de grâce* for the region came in 1981, when interest rates reached their highest ever level.

Table 6.1
Latin America: the most indebted region
The weight of the foreign debt, in Latin America and other developing countries

	Debt/export ratio [1]	Interest/GDP [2] (%)	Debt/GDP [3] (%)	Proportion of debt at floating interest rates [4] (%)
Latin America				
Argentina	4.3	7.7	47	34
Brazil	3.9	5.1	44	76
Chile	4.2	8.3	100	72
Venezuela	2.3	8.1	53	88
Other developing nations				
Algeria	1.3	2.8	24	21
Indonesia	1.2	1.6	35	23
Korea	1.5	2.2	37	42
Philippines	4.2	1.8	44	36
Nigeria	0.9	1.5	17	62

Sources: 1. 1983, World Bank; 2. Latin America, 1985, ECLAC; other developing nations, 1983, World Bank; 3. long-term debt only, 1984, World Bank; 4. 1983, World Bank.

But why did governments and countries in Latin America borrow so much more than the rest of the developing world at floating interest rates? Why did it take greater risks, practically giving the bankers a blank cheque?

Floating interest rates did not arise by chance, but as a mechanism that was required for the euromarket, that huge network of banks, situated outside the US, that held growing dollar deposits as a result of the post-war growth in trade. By passing on to the borrower the cost of any increase in interest rates, floating interest rates allowed banks to break one of the sacred rules of banking and make long-term loans with the backing of short-term deposits.

The emergence of the euromarket

The euromarket itself arose spontaneously, through a chance development. During the Second World War, the US Government lent money to the Soviet Union to boost the war effort, and at the end of the war, some was left over. Because of Soviet fears, in the worsening Cold War atmosphere, that these dollar reserves might be confiscated by the Americans, the Soviet Union preferred to keep them in European rather than US banks. So it was that the first dollar accounts were opened in European banks.

But this was only the tiny beginning of what was to grow into a huge new feature of the world financial market. The foreign investment boom that began in the 1950s among US transnationals created a heavy outflow of dollars from the US, reaching as much as $3 billion a year. Expanding world trade also absorbed more and more dollars. By 1960, net eurodollar deposits (that is, with relending subtracted) had already reached about $8 billion (*see* Table 6.2). This was equivalent to 14 per cent of official reserves in the whole of the capitalist world. But soon even this figure was to be dwarfed, with the constant rapid growth of dollar deposits outside the US.

Soon the practice of holding accounts outside the country of origin spread to other convertible hard currencies. The centre of the new market was London, where the number of subsidiaries of foreign banks grew rapidly, eventually reaching 365 in 1985, more than the total number of British banks (239). Other euromarket centres arose in Singapore, Bermuda, Nassau, the Cayman Islands and so on, with some of the markets offering tax enticements as well. It was a new financial system, based on tax havens and the idea of being outside the reach of national laws — almost a modern form of piracy.[3]

Banks from almost every country in the world, including Latin America, joined in the jamboree. New joint ventures arose, such as Eurobrás — an association between the Banco do Brasil, Bank of America, Deutsche Bank, Union des Banques Suisses and Dai-Ichi-Kangyo Bank, — created in 1972 to operate exclusively in the euromarket. But the US dominated, with 65 banks, representing 59 different banking groups, established in London.

The driving force behind the explosive growth was the rigidity of banking regulations in New York — the financial capital of the dollar empire which, paradoxically, did not play a direct role in the euromarket — and the other US financial centres. This inflexibility hardened in the 1960s, starting with resolution Q from the Federal Reserve Board (the Fed), which made it illegal for banks to pay interest on loans of less than 30 days, fixed at one per cent the interest to be paid on loans of up to 89 days, and at 2.5 per cent the interest on longer-term loans. This resolution led to a huge outflow of capital, as investors, just as surely as water flows downward, obeyed one of the basic rules of capitalism and sought a higher rate of return. In 1963, with the worsening of the American exchange crisis as a result of the outlay on the Vietnam war, the Fed introduced the interest equalisation charge, which taxed interest payments received from abroad by American residents or companies. It was yet another regulation that encouraged the outflow.

Some newspapers — and even academic works — refer to eurocurrencies as if they were some kind of special, mysterious currency. In reality, eurodollars are just ordinary dollars that are not subject to credit limitations or other Fed controls. 'There are only two places in the world where you can keep dollars, in a shoe box or in a US bank', commented the famous French economist, Jacques Rueff.[4] Even if they take a long and circuitous route via the euromarket, the dollars always end up back in the United States, the country where they were issued and where they have purchasing power. Even foreign central banks deposit their dollar reserves in American banks in the US. Those original Soviet dollar deposits, which gave birth to the euromarket, must eventually have found their way back to the US. But — and this was the crucial point for the Russians — these dollars were now regarded as assets of European banks and were thus given a high degree of protection from confiscation.

Dollars owned by individuals in small quantities may be kept in 'shoe boxes', but dollar credits owned by governments, companies and even rich individuals, necessarily end up in American banks in the US, even if the deposits are made originally in foreign subsidiaries of these banks. The same happens with eurofrancs, euromarks and eurosterling, all of which find their way eventually to banks inside the country of origin.

Table 6.2
The dollar's empire, beyond the law
The growth of the euromarket compared with that of official world reserves
($bn)

	Euromarket transactions			Official Reserves
	Gross	**Net of cross-lendings**	**Proportion in $ (%)**	
1960	10*	8	n.a	58.2
1965	30*	24	n.a	72.4
1970	110	65	81	92.3
1971	145	85	76	124.5
1972	200	110	73	158.7
1973	305	160	68	184.3
1974	375	215	71	222.2
1975	460	250	73	236.3
1976	565	310	74	258.6
1977	695	380	70	317.7
1978	895	485	74	320.0
1979	1,120	610	73	310.0*
1980	1,525	730	75	354.7*
1981	1,860	890	78	363.4*
1982	2,015	940	81	360.8*

* from IMF, International Finance Statistics, in DES.

Source: 1960-65, Morgan Guaranty, in Eugene L. Verluysen, *The Political Economy of International Finance*, St Martin Press, New York, 1981.

The term 'eurocurrency' or 'eurodollar' is essentially no more than an accounting trick, created by the banks, to allow unrestricted flows of hard currencies and to avoid the controls, often quite strict, that are placed on the money supply, above all on bank loans, in the country in which that currency is the local means of payment. The accounting invention arose for very simple reasons. Suppose a firm, a bank or an individual wanted to open a dollar account in the London subsidiary of a US bank, depositing a cheque or a money order. This cheque or money order could be made out against an account that the depositor had in the US, or it could be payment from a third party for a service performed or a trade transaction. In every case it had to be made out against some bank account in the US, as this is the only important country in the world in which the dollar is the national currency. The European subsidiary then informed its head company in the US of the deposit so that the transaction might be completed.

In the US, however, the total value of dollars deposited with the banks remained unaltered, for the cheque that had been originally issued had been deposited back in the country. But a dollar credit remained in the London bank. In the early days of the euromarket, banks invested in US treasury bonds or in comparable papers an equivalent amount of money to provide backing for these credits. These deposits earned interest.

Floating interest rates

Gradually, on the basis of these early deposits, backed up by treasury bonds, banks began to offer dollar loans to third parties. If the deposit was for a fixed term, the bank could make a profit with no risk by relending it for the same term at higher interest. But banks began to be asked for loans with a longer term than the six months for which the original deposits were made. The banks began to provide these loans, but only after the borrower had agreed to shoulder the whole risk by agreeing to have the interest on the loan re-assessed every six months, to bring it in line with market levels. It was in this way that the 'floating rate' clauses originated. As the market grew, the banks stopped providing backing for these credits, through investments in treasury bonds or equivalent papers. There was thus a net increase in the money supply.

The generalised adoption of floating rates, which introduced an extra element of freedom into the market, resulted at times in an anarchical situation, as was to be clearly demonstrated later by the debt crisis itself. But at the time bankers were not worried about a possible financial crisis in the future; they were caught up in the day-to-day problem of how to re-lend at a profit the huge volume of balance-of-payments surpluses that had resulted from the explosive growth in world trade, partly as a result of the rise in oil prices. And floating interest rates became an ideal mechanism for increasing profits substantially for the banks without involving them in an any additional risk. With floating interest rates, the whole risk of an increase in interest is transferred to the client, while the only risk for the bank is the final and definitive bankruptcy of the borrower, which at the time seemed a very remote possibility.

One of two rates was adopted as a reference point for the loan contracts: either prime rate, which already existed in the US and was the rate charged by the banks for their loans to their best customers; or the London Inter-Bank Offered Rate, known as Libor, which was created by the euromarket itself as the rate for lending between banks in the system. To prime or Libor was added an extra commission or an additional interest, known as the spread or margin, which varied on the whole between 1 and 2 per cent, according to the customer and the country, and which was presented by the banks as their profit in the operation. Borrowers had to pay the interest every six months, at the rate that prime or Libor had reached at that time, plus the spread.

At the time, prime was one of the main interest rates in the US. It reflected the general demand for credit which, in its turn, both influenced and was influenced by the Fed, which is constantly worried about the level of inflation in the US. The Fed openly manipulated interest rates on its treasury bonds, offering investors higher or lower levels depending on whether it wished to squeeze the market (to deflate the economy and bring down inflation) or, on the contrary, to increase liquidity to stimulate the economy. The interest paid on treasury bonds had an immediate impact on the negotiable certificates of deposit (CDs), the certificates issued by the banks to their clients for deposits. This is because the banks bought treasury bonds to absorb any excess liquidity from the sale of these certificates and would thus be unwilling to pay higher interest on their certificates than they were earning on the bonds. In turn, the interest paid on the CDs determined the level of interest to be charged on loans to large companies, that is, prime rate. So the rate of interest on the Fed's treasury bonds — an essential tool in US domestic policy-making — became the key element in determining the level of interest for loan contracts in eurodollars for Latin America.

Libor, in London, aligned itself with prime, almost always keeping a few points above it in order to attract US capital. While some fluctuations in prime and Libor were caused by Fed policies and by the general health of the US economy, seasonal fluctuations were determined by the demand for credit from the US corporations, which was generally lower in mid-winter, the December–January period.[5] But, as prime became increasingly adopted in floating interest loans to countries in the periphery, the system began to react and to adapt. Prime, which had been the lowest market rate, available only to big, reliable companies, became less and less used in the US itself. By 1981, over 60 per cent of the loans from the 48 largest banks to US corporations in the US were at rates less than prime.[6]

US transnationals, which had been used to raising money on the US market to be invested abroad, began in the 1960s to instruct their subsidiaries to find their own finance on the euromarket. Further restrictions from the Fed followed in later years, all of them indirectly encouraging the companies to turn to the euromarket and thus contributing to the disorderly and uncontrollable expansion of dollar transactions abroad.

In 1966, the subsidiary of the First National City Bank of New York issued in London the first negotiable certificate of deposit specially adapted to the needs of the transnationals. From then on all kinds of euro-certificates and euro-bonds were invented. By 1970 the gross value of euro-deposits was estimated at $110 billion, more than the total value of official reserves throughout the capitalist world. Five years later, the market had swollen to $250 billion, with the transnationals' share alone put at $30–35 billion.

Syndicated loans

In 1969, just after the invention of floating interest rates, the first syndicated loan was floated, at the initiative of the banker Minos Zombakis, to raise $80 million for Iran. The syndicated loan was a system by which a large number of banks could come together in a single loan operation. While floating interest rates allowed the banks to lend short-term money for long periods, almost without risk, syndicated loans let them put together far larger loans than would be thinkable for a single bank. At the high point of the recycling phase, when Latin America's financial needs had become insatiable, syndicated loans of as much as $1 billion were arranged in just a few days.

Syndicated loans were organised by a lead manager, who sent to 50 or more possible participants a telex, or placement memo, giving the conditions acceptable to the borrower, such as the term, reference interest rate and spread. One or two dozen banks would normally agree to take part with contributions of $1−10 million each. According to the bankers at the time, this kind of operation would reduce the risk for the big banks by allowing them to diversify their loan portfolios, scattering them among a wide variety of clients in a large number of countries, instead of putting all their eggs in one basket. And, so the argument went, it would also help the small banks by letting them take part in the boom, even if they knew nothing about Latin America, as they could rely on the judgement of the big banks in New York and London, some of which specialised in certain areas of the world.

Syndicated loans to Third World countries at floating interest rates dominated the financial market in the 1960s and 1970s. Big specialist publications drew up lists of the largest loans and ranked developing countries according to the spreads they were allocated by the bankers — a kind of financial 'Top of the Pops'. Hundreds of small and medium-sized banks throughout the world joined in the dance of the millions, lending to companies in countries they scarcely knew how to find on the map, guided only by the brief placement memo supplied by the lead manager.

The central banks in the industrialised countries never showed any interest in suppressing this market, or even in monitoring it. They claimed that transactions were carried out either in foreign currency, in which case they did not have a significant impact on the domestic money supply, or in the country's currency but abroad, thus limiting greatly their influence on the local market. In this way, a supra-national financial market and money supply were created, outside the control of any national monetary authority. In a short time this bubble-like market grew to an enormous size, overtaking the real markets from which it had arisen.[7]

'Eurocurrency' unmasked

The eruption of the debt crisis put an abrupt end to the myth of the 'stateless eurocurrency'. Overnight the simple underlying relation became clear for all to see: Latin America's real creditors were the big American banks in the USA, the big Japanese banks in Japan, the big German banks in West Germany and so on.

Though Latin American governments and companies have been greatly criticised in the West in recent years for their excessive borrowing, it must be said that at the time no alternative supply of funds was offered. The world financial institutions did not supply resources on anything like the required scale, and much of

Latin America was, in any case, considered to be too 'developed' to be an urgent priority. Moreover, commercial loans at floating interest rates seemed at the time to be a good bargain. With interest rates oscillating between 7 and 9 per cent and with world inflation at around 6−7 per cent, the Latin Americans ended up paying a real interest rate of only 1 or 0 per cent, or even, at times, less than zero, the so-called 'negative' rate of interest. One could scarcely ask for better rates than these, it would seem.

Always thinking in the short term and possessing unshakeable faith in the health of capitalism, Latin America's rulers were not aware that the downward phase in the long wave was commencing, a phase in which interest rates could increase brutally. Nor did they pay any attention to the monopolistic character of the financial market, dominated as it was by a few large banks that, within certain limits, had the power to manipulate interest rates. Nor were they concerned that the level of the floating interest rate that they were paying on their loans was established on the US money market and was largely determined by decisions taken by the Fed, usually with purely domestic considerations in mind.

By the late 1970s, the financial systems of the world were deeply intertwined, on a quite unprecedented scale, which meant that the crisis, when it eventually broke, was inordinately complex in terms of the financial mechanisms involved. With the eventual collapse of Mexico and Brazil, hundreds of small and medium-sized banks rapidly struck the whole of Latin America off the map, thus making the crisis even worse. The big banks, who could not afford to wipe out Latin America, did all they could to turn the continent into the prisoner of its own debt. It became clear that the euromarket, created to reduce risks, had in practice had the contrary impact, spreading the crisis widely throughout the developing world.

Notes

1. Article in *Foreign Affairs*, reproduced in *O Estado de S. Paulo*, 12 November 1985.
2. William Cline, *International Debt*, MIT Press, 1984.
3. See Jerry Coakley and Laurence Harris, *The City and the UK Economy*, Oxford, Basil Blackwell, 1984; and Hamish MacRae and Frances Cairncross, *Capital City*, Eyre Methuen, 1973.
4. *The Times*, 8 May 1974.
5. Charles R. Geisst, 'How issuers may use seasonal trends of Libor', *Euromoney*, June 1980.
6. Michael Moffitt, *O Dinheiro do Mundo*, Paz e Terra, 1985.
7. See Eugene L. Versluysen, *The Political Economy of International Finance*, New York, St Martin Press, 1981.

7. The American Solution to the Oil Crisis

How the industrialised centre transferred the oil bill to the periphery through dollar inflation, the deepening of the recession and an increase in interest rates

> . . . a country the size of the United States is never left without political resources.
> **Henry Kissinger**, *Business Week*, January 1975

The sudden increase in oil prices in January 1974 weakened the US economy even further, deepening its recession and spreading it throughout the other industrialised economies. The whole system began to suffer from a generalised and synchronised crisis.

The end of cheap energy

In a situation of near-panic, created by the oil embargo imposed on the US for its support of Israel in the Yom Kippur war, OPEC (the Oil Producing and Exporting Countries)[1] managed without any real difficulty to raise the average price of a barrel of oil from $2.80 to $9.46. This move meant the end of the very cheap energy which had sustained post-war prosperity and marked the beginning of an upturn in the fortunes of the oil-producing countries, which had earlier suffered from the successive dollar devaluations that had led to a fall in value of all goods quoted in dollars, not just those exported by the US.

Coffee-producing nations — Brazil, Colombia and the Ivory Coast — also tried at the same time to raise their income by forming a cartel, but their initiative failed. OPEC's success should be attributed in part to the important changes that were occurring in the oil industry. For the first time it became clear that the low-cost reserves in the Middle East, which had permitted voracious consumption and saturation selling, and had allowed the 'seven sisters', as the seven big transnational oil companies were called,[2] to wage a price war against the smaller producers, would not last indefinitely. The oil industry was moving on to high-cost drilling in the North Sea. This, on the one hand, demanded intensive capital investment, thus eliminating small producers, and, on the other, made the old oil price unrealistically low.[3] It was this transition towards capital-intensive oil extraction that created an opening for the Arab action, undertaken first by the revolutionary Libyan government in 1970, and then endorsed by the whole of OPEC.

Before the Arab initiative, more than half the retail price of a barrel of oil was appropriated by the governments in the consumer countries in the form of taxes and other charges. The transnational oil companies kept another 42 per cent, with only 6 per cent going to the country that produced the oil. From 1974 onwards, the producing countries began to retain a massive 34 per cent of the (now increased) income generated by a barrel of oil.[4]

Supplying two-thirds of the 46 million barrels of oil consumed every day by the western economies, OPEC members obtained an additional annual income of $60 billion. The US alone had to pay out an additional $17 billion a year, as it imported about half of the 18 million barrels it consumed every day. The US oil import bill jumped from $4.7 billion in 1972 to $26.2 billion in 1974 (and to almost $80 billion in 1980, when it accounted for a third of all US imports). Countries in the periphery (such as Brazil) that insisted on maintaining their fleets of individual cars instead of developing public transport, also suffered considerably.

It has been widely claimed, not least in the developing countries themselves, that the successive oil shocks were responsible for the Third World debt crisis. The US economist William Cline looked for empirical evidence to support this claim. His statistics suggest that 12 out of the 19 most heavily indebted developing countries would have saved $340 billion in the 1974−82 period, if oil prices had kept to their average level before the shock. The sum falls to $260 billion if it is assumed, perhaps more reasonably, that oil prices rose in line with the retail price index in the US. But, whichever figure is taken, the value is high. The lower figure is comparable with the total foreign debt — of $299 billion — contracted by these countries by the end of the period.[5]

The myth of the oil-induced debt crisis

But a closer look at what actually happened in the Third World does not support the claim that the increase in oil prices caused the debt crisis. Only three of the ten most-indebted developing nations — Brazil, India and South Korea — depended heavily on imported oil. If one adds another 25 countries to the list of the most-indebted developing nations, only three more countries — the Philippines, Pakistan and the Sudan — can claim that oil imports made a significant contribution to their indebtedness. Global oil figures, in fact, tend to conceal rather than to clarify the mechanism behind the debt trap.

Indeed, the countries most affected by the oil shock — and those that account for a large share of the additional outlay recorded by Cline — belong to the band of Mediterranean countries near the industrialised centre: Turkey, Greece, Israel, Portugal and Spain (as well as Yugoslavia, Hungary and Romania). Rather than creating insuperable debt problems for them, the oil crisis tended to strengthen these countries' links with the industrialised centre, removing them from the mass of Third World indebted countries.

It is true that Brazil and Uruguay paid a high price for the oil shock. Between the first increase in 1974, and 1982, Brazil paid $43.8 billion more than it would have done without the rise. About half of Brazil's debt can be attributed directly to the rise in oil prices. Even if oil prices had risen in line with the US retail price index, the additional outlay would have been $22.8 billion, in 1974 prices (*see* Table 7.1). Uruguay suffered as much as, or even more than, Brazil: in 1975 it used 44 per cent of its export earnings to import oil, more than any other Latin American country (*see* Table 7.2).

Table7.1
Oil and the Brazilian debt

How much the increase in oil prices cost the country

	Price of oil ($/barrel)[1]	Total outlay ($ bn)[2]	Excess outlay (nominal value) ($ bn)[3]	Excess outlay (deflated value) ($ bn)[4]
1973	2.6	0.654	—	—
1974	10.6	2.767	2.1	1.9
1975	10.6	2.699	2.1	1.7
1976	11.5	3.556	2.8	2.2
1977	12.3	3.753	2.9	2.2
1978	12.4	3.910	3.1	2.1
1979	17.1	6.218	5.2	3.2
1980	29.4	9.496	8.8	5.2
1981	34.4	9.674	8.9	4.5
1982	33.0	8.614	7.9	3.8
1983	29.4	6.789	6.2	2.8
1984	28.6	5.074	4.6	1.9
1985	28.0	3.614	3.1	1.3
Total			**57.7**	**28.8**

1. average price, FOB
2. outlay on imports of oil and derivates, minus re-exports
3. in nominal dollars, not corrected for inflation
4. corrected, from 1973 onwards, by US inflation

Source: Banco Central do Brasil

Table 7.2
Oil and the debt

The weight of oil and the weight of the debt, in the ten largest Latin American debtors

	Debt ($ bn)		Oil imports as % of total exports		Debt servicing as % of total exports	
	1973	1981	1975	1982	1973	1981
Brazil	13.8	75.7	36.4	53.0	36.7	66.9
Mexico	8.6	67.0	—	—	28.7	48.5
Argentina	6.4	35.7	13.4	7.5	19.9	37.5
Venezuela	4.6	29.3	—	—	3.8	19.0
Chile	3.6	15.0	16.4	16.0*	35.1	61.0
Peru	2.4	9.8	14.7	1.2	35.8	n.a.
Colombia	2.8	8.3	—	—	21.1	23.9
Bolivia	0.7	2.7	—	—	22.7	42.6
Ecuador	0.6	5.3	—	—	8.2	47.7
Uruguay**	0.4	1.8	44.0	32.0	22.0	13.4

* 1981 figure
** figures for Uruguay are approximate

Sources: IMF reports, 1978 and 1984, for oil imports; William Cline, *International Debt* (MIT Press, 1984), for debt service and total debt

But other important Latin American debtors — Argentina, Peru and Chile — were far less dependent on oil. In 1975, after oil prices had risen threefold, these countries were still only spending between 13 and 17 per cent of their export earnings on energy imports, largely oil. Another two nations on the list of the ten most indebted — Ecuador and Bolivia — are modest oil exporters. And two of the biggest nations — Mexico and Venezuela — were, and still are, important oil exporters, but still ended up high on the list of the most indebted. 'Mexico's large build-up of debt was almost certainly accelerated rather than deterred by higher oil prices', comments Cline. 'Mexico first borrowed heavily to develop oil production, and subsequently the promise of oil exports was the main basis for its ability to borrow large amounts.' Even in 1981, when oil prices reached their highest level — $31 a barrel — only Brazil among the big debtors and Uruguay among the small ones were really hurt. In that year they spent, respectively, 53 and 32 per cent of their export earnings on oil.

All these contradictions show that there is no clear line of causality between the rise in oil prices and indebtedness. Indeed, when the crisis arose, almost all the Latin American countries were already heavily indebted, allocating a large proportion of their export earnings to debt-servicing. Eight of the ten most indebted nations (the exceptions are Venezuela and Ecuador) were by then spending more than 20 per cent of their export earnings on debt-servicing. And, even at the height of the oil shock, all of them, even Brazil, spent more on debt-servicing than on oil imports.

Far more important than the rise in oil prices in itself was the response it provoked in the industrialised countries. It was the action taken jointly by industrialised countries to avoid bearing the full burden of the higher oil prices, by passing much of the cost on to the developing world, that greatly contributed to the acceleration of the Latin American debt crisis. This is not to say that the oil shock was unimportant, but merely to reassess its impact. It did not cause Latin America's debt crisis, but, directly and indirectly, it did reinforce it. During this period, the Brazilian and Mexican debts trebled, while the Latin American total more than doubled, to $130.8 billion in 1978.

Unlike the Great Depression in the 1930s, which culminated in a war between the world powers, the oil shock arose at a time when the economies of the three centres of power — the US, the European Economic Community (EEC) and Japan — were closely linked. Though the oil shock undoubtedly created tensions between the three blocs, it was the first real test of the new system. Could the three powers, in the midst of a nerve-racking crisis, find a solution that was acceptable to all three of them?

The defence of the industrialised centre

In the event, the new scheme came out well, for them. The crisis strengthened the organisations that had been set up for the exclusive defence of the countries in the industrialised centre, particularly the OECD (Organisation for Economic Co-operation and Development),[6] the body that brought together the 24 countries in the capitalist centre. At the initiative of the US Secretary of State, Henry Kissinger, the International Energy Agency was set up, with the participation of basically the same countries and with the exclusion of the Third World — even big oil consumers, such as Brazil and India. The Agency worked out plans for economising on energy and for developing alternative energy strategies so that the bargaining power of the OECD countries would increase with respect to OPEC. It also got its members to agree not to dump oil on the world market, so that the oil price would not fall below $8 a barrel, compromising the viability of investments into alternative sources of energy. World organisations such as the United Nations were weakened. It became more and more common for important world decisions to be taken at small 'summit meetings', sometimes involving just the two superpowers, on other occasions bringing together the 'Group of Five' capitalist nations (the 'Big Five' — US, Japan, West Germany, Britain and France). Just like the 'family' meetings of the US mafia, they involved the smallest number of people necessary for efficient decision-making.

The US Treasury had calculated that, if no corrective measures were taken, the OPEC countries would in five years accumulate an additional income of about $300 billion, three times the value of all US foreign investments. The World Bank's 1974 report warned that, if nothing was done to reverse this process, the OPEC countries would accumulate assets of $650 billion by the beginning of the 1980s and $1,200 billion by 1985. Overnight the industrialised countries had not only lost their annual surpluses of $20 billion that allowed them to finance the continual expansion of their economic empires, but had also started to run an annual deficit of $18 billion.

But, though they had suffered a temporary reverse, the industrialised countries were not prepared to give up permanently their traditional surpluses that were the result of historic terms of trade, originally established through the use of force. These surpluses necessarily generated deficits of the same size in the periphery countries, deficits that could be covered only by investments or loans from the rich countries — a process the IMF euphemistically called 'covering the current account deficit of the developing countries' and that the industrialised countries found highly profitable.

On the other hand, OPEC's additional yearly income represented only 1.6 per cent of the total economic output of the OECD countries ($2,420 billion in 1974) and 3.4 per cent of that of the US. NATO'S annual expenditure, at about $117 billion, was approximately three times the loss incurred by the OECD countries as a result of the new oil prices. In January 1974, the 20 most powerful countries in the IMF, the so-called 'Group of 20', met in Rome to see how they could redirect the flow of oil dollars — which they started to call 'petro-dollars' as if they were intrinsically different from other dollars.

All kinds of strategies were discussed at this meeting. It was even proposed that the countries should absorb the deficit through domestic programmes of economic adjustment. But such a policy would have entailed a permanent loss of income (something that was later to be demanded, on a much bigger scale, from the Latin American countries). But OPEC's strength was limited to the technical control of one commodity, without comparable economic and military back-up. It was scarcely to be expected that the industrialised countries would capitulate so easily.

The US government considered the use of force, but it did not receive the support of its European allies, who had special bilateral relations with some members of OPEC. After both domestic adjustment and armed action had been rejected, the only alternative was monetary manipulation, supported by a certain amount of political intimidation. 'The oil problem was to be resolved in the same way as the decline in the dollar was resolved: the world power of the US would guarantee its domestic maladjustment and basic structural questions would be resolved by external manipulation', wrote the US economist, David P. Calleo.[7] So once again the invisible but powerful arm of dollar hegemony was used. An arm that would hurt indiscriminately, not only OPEC countries, but also countries similarly located in areas of the world under the economic and financial domination of the dollar.

In monetary warfare, money — or liquidity — plays the part of ammunition. The first measure taken by the industrialised centre was to increase its own liquidity. The US government had already resorted to this device in 1970 when it wanted to relieve pressure on the dollar and prepare the way for the collapse in the gold standard. It had forced the European countries to accept the creation of Special Drawing Rights (SDRs), a kind of token used to settle accounts between governments and the IMF. On that occasion the allocation of SDRs depended on the number of quotas each particular country had in the IMF. In this way, it led to a general increase in liquidity, but benefited the wealthier countries, who had more quotas, far more than the poorer members.

But on this occasion the US government was hesitant. Despite the obvious benefits it would reap as the country with the largest gold reserves, it did not immediately accept the proposal from the French, Swiss and Italian central banks that the dollar value of official gold reserves should be increased fourfold. Since the beginning of the dollar crisis, the price of gold on the free market had soared, reaching $180 an ounce, four times the reference value in official reserves. The European banks wanted to use this gold as the Arabs had used oil. It was a measure that would benefit almost exclusively the industrialised countries. The Americans were reluctant because, as always, they wanted the best of all possible worlds. As they were no longer big gold producers, they did not want others to benefit, particularly the Soviet Union, believed to be the largest producer, and South Africa.

The abolition of the official price of gold

Finally, as the gap between market and official gold prices widened, the US was persuaded to abolish the official price. In December 1974, President Gerald Ford of the United States met President Giscard D'Estaing of France for a picnic in Martinique at which they worked out a scheme for de-regulating the price of gold without creating a fall in market prices — a problem that worried the gold-hoarding French. In the following year, the 'Big Five' met on the US President's yacht and decided to abolish the official price of gold, getting rid of the last plank of the Bretton Woods agreement. The value of official gold reserves, previously $45 billion, shot up overnight to $182 billion. The main beneficiaries were the US (who owned 27 per cent of these reserves), West Germany (11.6 per cent) and France (9 per cent). It was equivalent to a new devaluation of the dollar in relation to gold, and, like that, it meant in practice that the US Treasury short-changed its creditors.

Several proposals for increasing the liquidity of the periphery countries were also made, but all but one were turned down by the US. The exception was the decision, taken without even consulting OPEC, to use $6 billion of Arab money to create a special oil facility at the IMF to benefit non oil-producing developing countries.[8] But this was small beer, dwarfed by the measures taken by the industrialised countries to benefit themselves. A large emergency fund, worth $25 billion, was set up under the auspices of the International Energy Agency for the exclusive use of industrialised countries. According to David Calleo, Kissinger even considered it to be a 'moral insult' for any Third World country to demand a juster distribution of world wealth. In the speech about the US proposals for the oil crisis, read on his behalf in the United Nations' general assembly,[9] Kissinger refused to accept that the US was responsible for any of the difficulties that the world was experiencing. His answer to demands from developing nations for a new world economic order was to tell them to reap the benefits already available to them by opening up their economies completely to US capital. The same retort was to be made by Ronald Reagan ten years later.

The monetary solution to the Arab challenge would work, the US government hoped, as follows. By increasing world liquidity and thus feeding inflation, it would push up the dollar price of its export goods, particularly capital goods and armaments, where it was the world leader. If it could make the price of these goods grow even more rapidly than the price of oil, it would bring back the terms of trade to their pre-crisis levels. Simulations carried out by US banks showed that the OPEC countries would start to run a deficit once again in only five years, if their imports were to increase 20 per cent in volume and 12 per cent in price.[10] And, of course, as long as there was no further increase in the price of oil.

OPEC's limited capacity

But this strategy faced a serious obstacle: the limited capacity of the OPEC countries to absorb goods. The US Treasury calculated that 60 per cent of the $59 billion available to OPEC countries, once their usual imports had been made, belonged to countries with a small domestic market and thus incapable of absorbing significant quantities of goods: Saudi Arabia, the United Arab Emirates, Kuwait, Libya and Qatar. Three years later the US Treasury predictions were confirmed. The IMF's annual report stated: 'These countries, producing about half of the entire group's oil exports, but having only 3 or 4 per cent of its population, accounted for almost 90 per cent of the combined surplus in 1977.'[11]

That left Iraq, the fifth-largest oil producer, and Iran, the second-largest oil producer, which was already playing a key role in the USA's global military dispositions. With ambitious development plans, the authoritarian Shah Mohammed Reza Pahlavi had signed in 1972 a grandiose contract with the US, in which he expressed his intention to spend $15 billion over five years on the purchase of arms, factories and nuclear reactors. Indeed, the Iranian military budget was increased fivefold to $10 billion in 1975.[12] (After this came, first, the revolution, and then the long war with Iraq, with the industrialised countries secretly supplying arms to both sides. Though it arose too late to have an impact on the US strategy at this stage, the war would eventually encourage both sides to spend heavily and to hand back to the industrialised countries their excess dollars.)

Table 7.3

The American solution to the oil crisis

	1973	1974	1975–77 (annual average)	1978
1. The value of gold ($/ounce) quadruples	42.22	180	180	180
2. Inflation accelerates (average in seven largest capitalist economies)	8.8	12.2	11.8	9.0
3. The world economy stagnates. unemployment rate in:				
USA	4.9	5.6	7.5	6.1
West Germany	0.7	1.6	3.5	3.4
Great Britain	3.2	3.1	5.6	6.2
4. And interest rates float				
prime rate (USA)	8.8	11.2	6.9	9.7
Libor (London)	10.2	10.2	7.2	9.1
5. With the expansion of floating debt floating/total (%)	n.a.	27.2	49.0	59.1*
6. Latin America's interest bill rises	2.9	3.5	4.9	14.4
7. and the current account deficit transfers to the periphery: Current account:				
OECD	20.0	−19.0	−5.0	3.0
OPEC	7.0	68.0	37.0	62.0
Periphery countries	−11.0	−37.0	−36.0	−39.0
Latin America	−3.7**	−13.0	−11.7	−20.0

8. After three years of recession and inflation, the deficit of the rich countries is almost entirely transferred to the periphery countries.

*   for 1977
**   for Argentina, Brazil and Mexico
*** for 1979

Sources: IMF report 1985; Economic Report of the President 1985; *Conjuntura Economica; World Development Report.*

But the US still had to solve the problem of the surplus dollars held by the other five OPEC countries. Over half of the 'petrodollars' were invested in banks, particularly through the euromarket. At their meeting in Rome, the 'Big Twenty' had already suggested that these surpluses should be channelled to those developing countries capable of absorbing large volumes of goods and services — countries with large populations, such as Brazil, India and Mexico (which was not yet an important oil exporter). In this way, it was argued, demand for the goods produced by the industrialised countries would be increased. And so the idea of 'recycling' the petrodollars was born. It was a development that allowed periphery countries to pay more, not only for their oil, but also for capital goods and other products manufactured in the industrialised countries.

'During the first phase, the euromarkets can be the main channel [for the recycled dollars]. These markets are equipped to handle a large volume of funds, and have the flexibility and the confidentiality required by the lenders', said Jacques de Larosière, the managing director of the IMF. The catastrophic result that this policy was to have for the Third World was predicted as early as 1975 by Otmar Emminger, president of the OECD (and vice-president of the Bundesbank): 'Our latest projection suggests that, by around 1980, there will be one group of nations with very heavy debts, and another heavily in credit. Saudi Arabia alone should have some \$100 billion. But trading relations between the OECD, as a group, and OPEC countries should be balanced.'[13]

High inflation was required to allow the price of manufactured goods to rise quickly. Loosen the reins on inflation to invert the terms of trade: that was the thrust of US monetary policy (despite the fact that US inflation had been the initial cause of the whole crisis). Even at the best of times, the US government could not hold inflation under 2.5 per cent. It was the combined result of the transnationals' policy of automatically passing on any increase in costs, and of the expansion of financial capital. In times of war, inflation doubled. In the year before the first oil shock it had already leapt to a new record of 6.3 per cent, as a result of the Vietnam war, which was unpopular and could not thus be financed by a tax increase, and the devaluation of the dollar, which led many investors to exchange their dollar reserves for goods and raw materials. On top of all this, the Federal Reserve Board had allowed the money supply to grow excessively in an ill-fated endeavour to reflate the economy.

The oil shock came when the US economy was not only engulfed in a deeper recession than ever before, with falls in personal consumption, fixed investment and gross national product, but when it was also grappling with an inflationary upsurge. As the shock itself contained an inflationary component that the governments did not try to alleviate through a cut in taxes charged on petrol, inflation rose even higher. It was in this way that the economy began to suffer from 'stagflation', that perverse combination of stagnation with inflation that was to spread like an epidemic throughout the whole system.

In 1974, gross domestic product fell by 1.4 per cent in the US, 1.3 per cent in Japan and 1.6 per cent in Great Britain, and by an average of 0.7 per cent in the seven largest industrial powers. At the same time, inflation reached 9.6 per cent in the US and 12.2 per cent on average for the seven largest economies. Performance was similar in the following year: a fall of 0.7 per cent in the gross domestic product of the seven largest economies and average inflation of 11.8 per cent. For two years running, inflation reached double figures (*see* Table 7.3).

As a result of stagflation, the industrialised countries managed to claw back only a few points in their terms of trade, after losing 11 per cent in 1974. But they succeeded in scaring the OPEC cartel, so that, thoroughly frightened by the profundity of the world recession, it agreed to freeze the price of oil until 1978. The non oil-producing developing countries had to pay more for capital goods supplied by the industrialised countries and for some raw materials controlled by the transnationals, such as fertilisers. Their terms of trade fell 8 per cent in 1974 and another 13 per cent in 1975.

Interest rates rise

Much worse for Latin America than the fall in the purchasing power of its exports, which was temporarily and partially reversed by a surge in coffee prices following the 1975 frost in Brazil, was the first rise in interest rates. Stagflation made first prime rate and then Libor rise from 6.5−7 per cent just before the shock to 10−11 per cent in 1974. According to the conservative estimates of William Cline, the interest rate increase caused an immediate rise of $10 billion in the interest payable on the developing world's debt, then standing at $161 billion.

World interest rates fell for a time (1976−77), but this seemed only to whet the appetites of Latin American governments for further loans. Then came the new leap, to 14 or 15 per cent, and Latin America's debt began to snowball out of control. The growing current account deficits were covered by new loans, always at floating interest rates. This increased the principal, which in turn pushed up the interest bill and forced the countries to increase their borrowing yet further, to the satisfaction of the IMF.

> In recent years the international capital markets, particularly the international banking system, have played a very active and effective part in recycling funds from countries with current account surpluses to countries in deficit . . . in 1976 and again in 1977, a number of non-oil primary producing countries borrowed substantial sums in the international credit markets. . .[14]

By 1978, the US strategy seemed to be working, in the short term at least. Much more through extracting interest like a usurer than through obtaining higher payments for goods, the industrialised countries managed to transfer almost the whole cost of the oil shock to periphery countries imprisoned by the trap of floating interest rates. The current accounts of the three blocs — the industrialised countries, OPEC and non oil-producing developing countries — had readjusted almost exactly as Otmar Emminger had predicted. Showing little concern for the predicament of the deficit countries, the IMF, which was supposedly created to help eliminate imbalances in international financial flows, said cynically in its annual report:

> It seems likely, therefore, that renewed deterioration of the terms of trade of non oil-exporters will be a major feature of 1978 world and payments developments. The major oil exporters comprise another group of countries whose terms of trade are destined to deteriorate in 1978, because of the continuation of the present price freeze of the Organisation of Petroleum Exporting Countries through the end of the year. The corresponding terms of trade gains will accrue mainly, of course, to the industrial countries.[15]

The way out found by the US from the first oil shock may have brought it temporary gains, but only at the price of deepening the country's own crisis. 'Just as the inflation of the dollar in the early 1970s fed world inflation, encouraging and intensifying the explosion in oil prices, so the inflationary US solution for the oil crisis led to a new explosion in world inflation', said David Calleo.[16] He pointed to the increased liquidity which put direct pressure on prices in the US, where the general consumer price index rose by a record 13.3 per cent in 1979.

Notes

1. The countries in OPEC are: Algeria, Ecuador, Gabon, Indonesia, Iran, Iraq, Kuwait, Libya, Nigeria, Qatar, Saudi Arabia, United Arab Emirates, Venezuela.

2. The 'Seven Sisters' are today six: Exxon, Mobil, Socal (controlled by the Rockefeller family), British Petroleum, Shell and Texaco. With strong links between them, they controlled two-thirds of production and half of the installed capacity for refining in the western world in 1974.

3. It consisted of the transition from a regime of decreasing marginal costs to one of growing marginal costs, to use the economists' jargon.

4. M. Jaidah, *OPEC Review*, June 1977.

5. William Cline, *International Debt*, MIT Press, 1984.

6. The following countries belong to the OECD: USA, Japan, Turkey, Australia, New Zealand, Canada and the whole of Western Europe.

7. David P. Calleo, *The Imperious Economy*, Harvard University Press, 1982.

8. Even so, the OPEC countries lent on average $5 billion a year at concessionary interest rates. See 'The OPEC Aid Record', Papers on the Economics of Oil, Oxford University Press, 1979.

9. Read by the US representative at the UN, Daniel Moynihan, and reproduced in its entirety by the *New York Times*, 2 September 1975.

10. Projections by Morgan Guaranty Trust, Irving Trust and First National City Bank, and by Walter Levy, made between January and June 1975.

11. IMF annual report, 1978.

12. For the Shah's plans, see Ahmed Faroughy and Jean-Loup Reverier, *L'Iran contre le Cha*, Jean-Claude Simoen, 1979.

13. *Guardian*, 15 March 1975.

14. IMF annual report, 1978.

15. IMF annual report, 1979.

16. David P. Calleo, op.cit.

8. Financial Seduction

Four cautionary tales: how the bankers entrapped Mexico, Brazil, Chile and Argentina

> Ideas, knowledge, science, hospitality, travel — these are the things that of their nature should be international. But let goods be homespun, whenever it is reasonably and conveniently possible, and, above all, let finance be primarily national.
> **J.M. Keynes**, in the *Yale Review*, 1933

'Brazil competes with Japan as the fastest-growing economy in the world. As it has charmed the international financial community, bankers feel so happy in lending money to Brazil, happier than elsewhere, that it has even been necessary to bridle them.' This was the beginning of an article about the 'Brazilian miracle' in *The Banker*, the London bankers' magazine, in February 1974, in the middle of the oil crisis. It was a serious article which, despite its enthusiasm for Brazil, warned its readers that most loans made to Latin America were at floating interest rates. 'Brazil will be hostage to the destiny of the eurodollar', it cautioned.[1]

But the readers of *The Banker* did not want to listen. With the industrialised world in deep recession, the bankers, who were awash with money from US investors and the Arab countries, began to court Latin American officials. It did not turn out to be a difficult task: 'It was the easiest money going',[2] one London banker recalled. 'You took 1 per cent on the turn, for signing a cheque for a few million dollars'. And, even without the extra lure of great personal gain from the bribes that were frequently paid, the offers were tempting for the Latin American governments. A former Latin American finance minister said: 'I remember how the bankers tried to corner me at conferences to offer me loans. If you are trying to balance your budget, it's terribly tempting to borrow more money instead of raising taxes.'[3]

Some analysts have dismissed all involved, borrowers and creditors, as idiots. 'Stupid bankers made stupid loans to stupid countries' was how one observer put it.[4] But this is to ignore the perverse logic of the scheme. The set-up enabled the banks to make unprecedented profits out of Latin America. It was evident from the beginning that the scheme could not last indefinitely, but the close integration of Latin America's ruling elites within the international financial system made it unlikely that they would ever opt for the repudiation of the debt or any other radical action. And, to oil the wheels of the whole operation, the bankers connived in massive capital flight that bound the ruling elites ever more firmly to the western banking system.

Far from stupid, the bankers played a clever, premeditated game. Though even by the mid-1970s, loans to developing countries accounted for a relatively small share of the total lending of the big US money-centre banks, their contribution to profits was much greater. At the Bank of America, profits from international lending rose from 21 per cent of the total in 1972 to 40 per cent of the total in 1976. In Manufacturers Hanover and J.P. Morgan, they accounted for over 50 per cent, and in Citibank and Chase Manhattan, for over 70 per cent.[5] Brazil alone yielded 20 per cent of Citibank's profits while absorbing only 5 per cent of its assets. Even at the time, Latin American economists complained that these high rates of profit amounted to discrimination.

It was evident too that commercial loans were particularly unsuited to Latin America's needs. In their lending to developing countries, the banks were interested above all in a high rate of profit as quickly as possible, to try to offset harmful developments in the industrialised countries, particularly the excess liquidity that had brought interest rates down and reduced the banks' spreads (that is, the extra interest charged by the banks to cover their costs and provide them with profit). 'Interest rates are being dangerously reduced . . . There are banks paying high rents in the City who are prepared to lend to anyone to cover their current expenditure', complained one banker in the magazine *Euromoney*.[6]

But what Latin America really required was not expensive loans at floating interest rates, but long-term finance, with fixed low interest rates, that could be invested in development projects. As the US economist Albert Fishlow has pointed out, commercial bankers were, paradoxically, much more prepared to lend to developing countries that did not need the money than to those that did. 'Harmfully, lack of need facilitates access to capital', he wrote. 'It is easier to obtain loans to build up reserves than to import, easier to obtain loans when you have an excess of foreign currency rather than a shortage.'[7]

Moreover, as well as insisting that their lending to the developing world should be carried out at floating rates of interest, the banks always fixed the other, less important rules to serve their interests. For instance, they were firmly opposed to the repayment of loans ahead of schedule. If a country had been able to take advantage of improved conditions on the world market to raise new loans to pay off old ones, it would have saved that country money, but the banks' profits would have been reduced. To prevent this, the banks resorted to two courses of action: they wrote special clauses into the loan contracts instituting penalties for early repayments, as was the case with 60 per cent of the medium-term loans contracted by Peru from the commercial banks between 1971 and 1976;[8] or they used 'moral persuasion', that is, threatened the borrowers with reprisals, as apparently happened to Brazil when, in 1978, it showed interest in getting rid of some particularly burdensome loans.[9]

But if, on the contrary, a country faced balance of payments difficulties, the banks rarely agreed to roll over old loans, that is, postpone the repayment of principal while continuing with the old conditions and terms. They almost always insisted on negotiating new loans, with very short terms and high spreads and fees. Apart from increasing profits, this strategy allowed the banks to keep the debtor nation on a 'short lead', making it more sensitive to outside pressure in its economic decision-making.

Despite these numerous disadvantages to commercial loans, almost all Latin American nations, most of which were ruled over by unresponsive and unelected military dictatorships, gave in to the temptation and so lost a rare chance to break out of the debt trap. As part of the US 'monetary solution' to the oil shock, commodity prices rose. Despite the difficulties caused to some Latin American nations by the higher oil prices, Latin America could have restricted imports and used part of its export earnings — which rose from $15.4 billion in 1971 to $40 billion in 1974 — to pay off part of the debt.But the opportunity was not seized. Dazzled by the abundant credit, tempted by the low interest rates (which gave the impression that the money was being lent free of charge), and seduced by the chance to amass huge fortunes abroad, Latin America's rulers took the easy option, contracting more and more loans precisely when the crisis was deepening. Shrewd observers, such as Lord Harold Lever, economic adviser to the Wilson government, warned repeatedly in the late 1970s that the whole house of cards would soon come tumbling down. When pressed, many bankers generally admitted that the whole scheme was very precarious. But they also knew that it would be the debtors, not themselves, who would be first to suffer. As, indeed, we shall show in our tales of the continent's four leading debtors — Mexico, Brazil, Chile and Argentina.

Mexico: oil and dissipation

The extreme case was clearly Mexico, which had just discovered new, abundant oil reserves and should, one would imagine, have been embarking on a new phase of solid economic development. When he took office in 1976, President López Portillo inherited a financial crisis from his predecessor, Luís Echeverría. After two years of austerity, López Portillo abandoned the painful course of structural change. Instead of pushing ahead with the difficult reforms in the financial, industrial and farming sectors that were required to put the economy on a sound footing, he opted for the much easier course of attracting into the country a huge influx of foreign loans to develop the oil industry.

In 1977, Jorge Díaz Serrano was appointed head of the state oil company, Pemex, and he set about expanding the country's oil output at a frenetic pace. A faction within the government pressed for slower development so that local industry would be able to supply most of the equipment and thus gain some benefit. But this advice was ignored, as development fever gripped the president and his top aides. Crude oil production rose from 1.2 million barrels a day in 1978 to 2.8 million in 1982. The volume of oil exports rose by about 40 per cent a year, while the value soared even more spectacularly, as a result of the boom in oil prices. Oil export earnings, which had been less than $2 billion in 1977, rose to almost $16 billion in 1978, the year of the second oil shock.

Borne along on this enormous wave of oil, Díaz Serrano set up a virtually independent fiefdom, fixing his own policies and spending money as lavishly as he thought fit. It is even said that, to boost his investment budget, he deliberately misled the president into believing that Mexican refineries could handle the heavy oil in the offshore reserves in the Gulf of Mexico — which they could not. Once brought into production, this oil became an embarrassing white elephant which could not be used at home and was in little demand elsewhere.[10]

During the oil boom, the economy grew by over 8 per cent a year, creating several million jobs. Heavy investments were made in hydroelectricity and IMF loans were paid off ahead of time. Hailed throughout the industrialised world as a remarkable success story, Mexico attracted hordes of foreign bankers, who were falling over themselves to lend, but relatively little foreign investment from the transnationals. From the end of 1978 to mid-1982, foreign investment totalled $7.3 billion, compared with a remarkable influx, of $54.4 billion, in foreign loans. How were all these loans spent?

Table 8.1
Mexico: The flow of resources
(US$ billions)

	1977	78	79	80	81	82	83	84	85	86
Outflow										
Net services (total)(a)	1.0	1.6	2.8	5.6	10.2	12.5	8.7	9.1	8.3	6.4
interest	1.0	1.5	2.3	3.7	5.8	9.8	8.8	9.7	8.8	7.5
others	0.2	0.1	0.5	1.9	4.4	2.7	0.7	−0.8	−0.5	−0.9
Amortisation* (b)	4.0	5.8	9.1	7.7	7.5	3.3	3.0	5.7	5.5	4.5
Other outflows** (c)	4.3	3.9	1.2	3.8	11.7	12.8	7.3	5.2	3.9	2.0
Total (d=a+b+c)	9.3	11.3	13.1	17.1	29.4	28.6	19.0	20.0	17.7	12.9
Inflow										
Loans (e)	10.4	12.6	14.9	18.7	31.7	16.7	6.8	8.6	6.6	8.2
Foreign investment (f)	0.5	0.8	1.3	2.2	2.5	1.3	0.5	0.4	0.5	0.9
Total (g=e+f)	10.6	13.4	16.2	20.9	34.2	18.0	7.3	9.0	7.1	9.1
Net transfer										
(h=g−d)	**1.3**	**2.1**	**3.1**	**3.0**	**4.8**	**−10.6**	**−11.7**	**−11.0**	**−10.6**	**−3.8**
(h=i+j)										
Achieved through:										
Trade balance*** (i)	1.0	1.7	2.8	2.8	4.1	−6.8	−13.7	−12.8	−8.4	−4.6
Net change in reserves**** (j)	0.3	0.4	0.3	1.0	0.7	−3.8	2.0	1.8	−2.2	0.8

*   It covers amortisation of all long- and medium-term debt for 1977, 1978, 1979, 1980 and 1981. Figures for amortisation of private debt are not available for 1982, 1983 and 1984, but they are known to have involved small sums.

** This figure is residual and is calculated according to the methodology described in Table 2.1.

*** A trade surplus is represented by a minus sign as it indicates a flow of resources out of the region.

**** A decrease in reserves is indicated by a minus sign, as it indicates a flow of resources out of the region.

Sources: 1. IDB annual reports; 2. ECLAC annual reports; 3. World Debt Tables, World Bank; 4. Calculated from ECLAC's annual figures for gross foreign debt and the World Bank's amortisation figures.

Some were used to cover the yawning trade deficit (*see* Table 8.1). Despite the rapid growth in exports, which increased from $4.6 billion in 1977 to $19.9 billion in 1981, they were outpaced by imports, which soared from $5.6 billion to $24.0 billion in the same period. The surge was partly a result of the industrial expansion plan, which led to a big increase in the purchase of foreign machinery and equipment, and partly as a consequence of the overvalued peso, which made imported consumer goods appear cheap and encouraged Mexicans to spend holidays in the US. The government was reluctant to devalue the peso, as it would have increased the cost of imported foodstuffs, particularly grains, upon which Mexico was becoming increasingly dependent because of the poor state of the neglected farm sector.

But, apart from encouraging Mexicans to travel abroad and, just as important, discouraging Americans from visiting Mexico, the overvalued peso had another unfortunate consequence: it tempted Mexicans to invest abroad, particularly in property in the US, which became relatively cheap. Private groups, like Alfa, expanded by borrowing money abroad, not by ploughing back profits. These were distributed to shareholders, who began to invest heavily abroad. With a 3,000-kilometre border with the US, it would have been extremely difficult for the Mexican government to impose rigorous exchange controls had it wished to do so. As it was, it made little attempt. Capital flight became rife, probably totalling \$2 − 3 billion each year from 1977 to 1980 and exceeding \$10 billion in both 1981 and 1982, a period in which confidence in the Mexican economy drained away.

Lavish spending, capital flight and conspicuous consumption were rife. ' "*Derroche*", defined in the dictionary as "dissipation, waste, squandering and destruction" is one of the two words which history will probably use to define the six-year government of President López Portillo', wrote one seasoned observer of Mexico. (The other word is 'oil'.)[11]

Uncontrolled, the foreign debt rapidly snowballed. The share of new borrowing used simply to pay back old debts and to pay the interest rose from the already high level of 51 per cent in 1977 to 76 per cent in 1979. It is extraordinary to note that, although Mexico borrowed \$88 billion between 1976 and 1981, the country received a net transfer of just \$14.3 billion. Almost all of the rest was either spent in servicing the debt itself (\$48.6 billion) or wasted in capital flight (\$24.9 billion).

Brazil: the debt of the miracle

The largest debt in Latin America was born of an alliance between the local bourgeoisie and foreign capital, an almost perfect example of growth under authoritarianism, in which corruption and capital flight were relatively unimportant, compared with the insuperable contradictions of the model itself.

The monetarists, headed by Roberto Campos, who came to power with the military coup of 1964, were charmed by the bankers and defined the opening of the country to foreign capital as one of the main planks of the new economic policy. It was plainly stated in the new government's Plan for Economic Action:

> The basic objective of our foreign capital policy is to speed up the economic development of the country through the use of foreign resources. The insufficiency of domestic savings to carry out the volume of investment required by our development programme makes

foreign technical and financial assistance indispensable.

The ground had been prepared by two years of intense recession that bankrupted hundreds of companies and paved the way for the 'economic miracle', a long period of rapid growth such as rarely occurs in capitalist economies and had never before occurred in Latin America. Miracles like this one had happened only twice before in the post-war period: in Japan and in West Germany. In both countries, the same two factors had made the miracle possible: cheap labour, the result of mass migration from East Germany into West Germany, and the total subordination of the Japanese worker to his boss; and foreign markets for the goods produced.

Table 8.2
Brazil: The flow of resources
($ bn)

	1977	78	79	80	81	82	83	84	85	86
Outflow										
Net services (total)(a)	5.0	5.9	7.7	10.1	13.2	16.1	13.4	13.2	12.9	12.5
interest	2.2	3.0	4.8	6.9	9.4	11.9	9.5	10.5	11.2	10.3
others	2.8	2.9	2.9	3.2	3.8	4.2	3.9	2.5	1.7	2.2
Amortisation*(b)	3.7	5.2	6.5	6.8	7.3	7.3	3.4	2.9	2.5	3.0
Other outflows** (c)	2.5	1.7	1.3	1.6	0.0	1.0	2.9	0.7	4.5	6.3
Total (d=a+b+c)	11.2	12.8	15.5	18.5	20.5	24.4	19.7	16.8	19.9	21.8
Inflow										
Loans (e)	10.1	16.7	13.1	16.3	17.7	16.3	9.9	7.1	5.6	8.9
Foreign investment(f)	1.7	1.9	2.2	1.5	2.3	2.4	1.4	1.5	1.3	1.0
Total (g=e+f)	11.8	18.6	15.3	17.8	20.0	18.7	11.3	8.6	6.9	9.9
Net Transfer										
(h=g−d) (h=i+j)	**0.6**	**5.8**	**−0.2**	**−0.7**	**−0.5**	**−5.7**	**−8.4**	**−8.2**	**−13.0**	**−11.9**
Achieved through										
Trade balance*** (i)	0.1	1.2	2.7	2.8	−1.2	−0.8	−6.5	−13.1	−12.5	−8.3
Net change in reserves**** (j)	0.5	4.6	−2.9	−3.5	0.7	−4.9	−1.9	4.4	−0.5	−3.6

*   It covers amortisation of all long- and medium-term debt for 1977, 1978, 1979, 1980, 1981 and 1982. Figures for amortisation of private debt are not available for 1983 and 1984, but they are known to have involved small sums.
**   This figure is residual and is calculated according to the methodology described in Table 2.1.
*** A trade surplus is represented by a minus sign as it indicates a flow of resources out of the region.
**** A decrease in reserves is indicated by a minus sign, as it indicates a flow of resources out of the region.

Sources: 1. IDB annual reports; 2. ECLAC annual reports; 3. World Debt Tables, World Bank; 4. Calculated from ECLAC's annual figures for gross foreign debt and the World Bank's amortisation figures.

These factors were also present in Brazil, though the external market was less important, particularly in the early years. Its cheap labour stemmed from the massive rural exodus that had taken place as labour-intensive crops, such as coffee, were pushed out by mechanised crops, such as soyabeans. The traditional forms of share-cropping ceased to exist and peasant families, who had previously been allowed to live on the large estates, were evicted. At the height of the 'miracle' in 1970, 29.5 million Brazilians, mostly rural workers, no longer lived in the place where they had been born. It was a repetition, on a much vaster scale, of the enclosures in medieval England that preceded the industrial revolution.

At the time that these changes were taking place in the countryside, workers were being repressed in the cities. Two big strikes were broken, one in Osasco (São Paulo), one in Contagem (Minas Gerais). Congress was closed down and opposition leaders, including leading economists from ECLA's structuralist school, such as Celso Furtado, were forced into exile.

Job security was abolished, allowing companies to sack long-established workers and to replace them with others on lower wages. The minimum wage, which is the basic wage of half the work-force and was already low, fell by 25 per cent in three years. Average wages in industry fell by 10 per cent. At the same time, a privileged middle-class sector, made up of people in the professions, executives and civil servants, grew rapidly. The share of national income going to the richest 5 per cent increased from 27.7 per cent in 1960 to 34.8 per cent in 1970. By 1976 it had grown to almost 40 per cent. At the same time, the poorer half of the population saw its share dwindle, from 17.7 per cent in 1960 to 14.9 per cent in 1970.

Once this income polarisation had taken place, it was not difficult to spark off a boom through the expansion of banking credit, caused partly by the conversion of foreign loans. With cheap, abundant labour, a high level of idle capacity as a result of the earlier recession, and an expanding elite, keen to consume, all the conditions were propitious. The recovery began in civil construction, which was able to employ unskilled labourers evicted from the countryside to build the homes needed by the new elites and the emerging middle class. It spread to manufacturing, particularly consumer durables, and then to the economy as a whole.

The military regime took several measures to facilitate the inflow of foreign capital. As early as August 1964, it substituted law no. 4,309 for no. 4,131, simplifying the procedures by which the subsidiaries of transnationals could bring foreign currency into the country. In 1967 the Central Bank introduced resolution 63, allowing the local investment banks to borrow money on the euromarket at floating interest rates and to pass on these loans in national currency to national companies. At the same time, it introduced the system of crawling-peg devaluations, by which the exchange rate was adjusted each week, according to the difference between Brazilian and US inflation. This favoured exports and reduced the risk of a maxi-devaluation. It was a set of measures that internationalised Brazil's credit system, linking it closely to the volatile eurodollar market.

Big, medium-sized and even tiny companies, like the baker's on the corner, were persuaded by bank managers to take out loans 'under 63' as they said, or loans for which you had to pay commissions and which would be affected, not only by the exchange rate, but also by interest fluctuations on the euromarket. Few people had even heard of prime and Libor, for it was not until after the first oil shock that the Central Bank began to include them in their statistics. But people agreed to accept these loans, largely because at the zenith of the Brazilian 'miracle', from 1969 to 1972, '63' loans were relatively cheap, as Libor had dropped to less than 7 per cent, which meant a real interest rate of only 1 per cent (though the spread and commissions had to be added to this). In their turn, exporters were offered a generous mix of fiscal and credit incentives.

During the six years of the 'miracle', the gross foreign debt more than tripled, from $3.9 billion in 1968 to $12.6 billion in 1973. The snowballing of the debt began effectively during this period. The proportion of GDP required for debt servicing rose from 2 per cent in 1968 to 3 per cent by 1973, a large absolute increase as the GDP itself had doubled in this period.

The 'miracle', particularly the new role played by the transnationals, began to erode Brazil's external accounts. Taking advantage of the new facilities, the transnationals substituted loans for equity. Their share of Brazil's foreign borrowing rose from 18.2 per cent at the beginning of the 'miracle' to 42.8 per cent at the end.[12] From 1969 to 1973, they were responsible for 60 per cent of the $10 billion borrowed by the country as a whole. The money was really disguised investment, brought in as loans to enable the companies to pay less income tax. Unlike remittance of dividends, remittance of interest was not charged income tax, and could also be discounted from taxable income. The subsidiaries of transnationals also began to import more goods from their head companies. Imports of non-ferrous metals, fertilisers and other intermediary products began to weigh heavily on the trade balance. In 1971, Brazil ran a trade deficit — of $400 million — for the first time in a decade. In all, it has been calculated that, if one includes all their outlays in foreign currency, including their imports, by 1975 the 115 largest transnational companies in Brazil were responsible for an annual net deficit of no less than $1.7 billion.[13]

Despite the claims made in the Plan for Economic Action, the euro-loans did not have an essential role, either as a source of foreign exchange or as 'foreign savings'. Domestic savings grew from 14 to 20 per cent of GDP during the period, quite sufficient by themselves to fuel growth. It is estimated that only 25 per cent of productive investments were financed by long-term or medium-term external capital.[14] It was a signficant contribution, but by no means indispensable.

Indeed, much of the foreign borrowing was quite unnecessary, as can be seen from the fact that seven out of every ten dollars borrowed abroad remained as a deposit with the creditor bank, entirely otiose. International reserves grew from $300 million in 1968 to $6.4 billion in 1974. As we will show later, there is considerable evidence that government officials in Brazil, and in other Latin American countries in the charge of monetarists, were so dominated by foreign bankers that they acted as an overspill for the euromarket, borrowing to relieve the banks of excess liquidity, rather than in response to their own country's balance of payments requirements. Allowing for a time lag, economists have traced a close correlation between the level of Brazil's reserves and low points in interest rates on the euromarket. By comparing the interest that Brazil was paying on its loans with the interest it was receiving on its reserves, it can be seen that, by holding such absurdly high reserves, enough to pay for a whole year's imports, Brazil lost, in a single year, about $120 million.[15]

Grandiose and inessential projects were undertaken with the foreign funding: the Transamazonian highway, the Rio—Niteroi bridge and the Angra 1 nuclear power station are the best known. Apart from the power station, none of these projects required foreign funding. Imports of capital goods grew slowly, far more slowly than imports of durable consumer goods.

The last reason given in the Plan for Economic Action to justify foreign borrowing was 'indispensable technical assistance from abroad'. This also was far less effective than had been imagined. The most spectacular of the projects involving imported technology — the ambitious nuclear deal signed with West Germany — was expanded in the late 1970s, but then ended in disaster, with the construction of only two of the nine reactors planned. There is even some evidence that the bankers suspected this from the beginning. 'Standards for assessing loans are low, with often basic principles being ignored', said a director at the Bank of London and South America.[16]

The supply of loans to Brazil became so intense that, in October 1972, the Central Bank introduced a compulsory deposit, of 25 per cent, on all foreign borrowing. Eight months later this restriction was replaced by a ban on loans with a repayment period of less than ten years. Then, at the beginning of 1973, the Central Bank reintroduced the compulsory deposit, fixing it this time at 40 per cent, while retaining the ban on loans with a repayment period of less than ten years.

None of these changes was important. What the Central Bank failed to realise was that, with floating interest rates, the repayment period was irrelevant. Whether the loan was long-term or short-term, all the risk was taken by the client. Instead of merely insisting on long maturities, the Central Bank should have made it impossible for development projects, where long-term finance was required, to be funded by loans with floating interest rates. For it was evident that the longer the term, the greater the probability that interest rates would exceed the project's planned rate of return and jeopardise its whole financial viability. Long-term projects could be safely financed only by long-term loans at fixed interest rates, or with clauses that in some way limited or restricted interest fluctuations.

The 'miracle' strengthened relations between the big state companies, the citadels of the military bureaucracy, which had expanded their activities in the basic sectors of the economy, and the transnationals dominating the finished product sector. It was a new form of the old alliance between Latin American elites and foreign capital. Ordinary people were once again excluded from the benefits. Infant mortality, that classic method for measuring social well-being, actually increased significantly in some cities during the 'miracle' years. In São Paulo, the number of deaths of babies less than one year old rose from 74.3 per 1,000 live births in 1967 to 89.5 in 1974.[17]

The new President-General, Ernesto Geisel, who took office in March 1974, deliberately ignored both the very special shock that Brazil received from the rise in world oil prices, and the signs that the world economy was heading for recession. Bringing together state companies with European and Japanese groups, he drew up an ambitious development plan for basic industries to try to eliminate the bottlenecks left by the consumerist style of expansion experienced during the 'miracle' years and, in this way, to push the economy into a new leap forward. A large number of big new projects was undertaken at the same time: steel mills (Tubarão and Açominas), hydroelectric power stations (Itaipu, the largest in the world, and Tucuruí), railways, aluminium refineries in the Amazon, a copper refinery in the north-east, capital goods factories, petrochemical complexes and a vast nuclear programme, with nine large plants and the whole fuel cycle. It was the most ambitious development programme ever undertaken by the country, comparable with the great industrialisation drives undertaken in the USSR and China, but with far fewer sacrifices. It was said that a new and painless short cut to industrialisation had been discovered. The abundant foreign finance was seen as a gift from heaven. Brazil would experience rapid growth, precisely at a time when almost every other country was facing recession.

At first, it seemed as if Geisel's strategy was working. With wages still very low, and with some projects begun during the last phase of the 'miracle' coming on stream, manufactured exports began to grow. The trade deficit, which had reached \$4.7 billion in 1974, the first full year of the oil shock, dropped repeatedly, until it was all but eliminated in 1977. But, while the trade account improved, the capital account deteriorated — Latin America's old story of financial bleeding. By 1977, profit remittances reached \$500 million and interest payments much more, \$2.2 billion. Almost imperceptibly, Brazil was being sucked into the debt trap. In 1977, almost 60 per cent of the country's record level of new borrowing of over \$10 billion, was spent on debt-servicing (*see* Table 8.2).

The foreign debt had already almost tripled, from around \$18 billion at the beginning of the Geisel government to over \$48 billion in 1978. And then Brazil suffered simultaneously two more shocks — the second rise in oil prices, which caused big trade deficits, of \$1.2 billion in 1978 and \$2.7 billion in 1979; and the increase in interest rates on the euromarket, which increased interest payments to \$3.0 billion in 1978 and to the much higher figure of \$4.8 billion in the following year. The difference between the amount Brazil received from abroad in exports and what it had to pay out in imports and debt-servicing was now over \$10 billion a year. It was a structural deficit that could be reduced only through big reductions in investment and a profound recession.

But foreign loans had already become a crutch for the government and, above all, for the big state companies, which by now did not know how to survive without them. Loans for the public sector, brought in under law 4,131, which had accounted for only 25 per cent of the borrowings in 1972, increased their share to 76 per cent in 1979. The scheme suited the federal government too, because it indirectly provided hard currency for debt-servicing, and commercial banks always preferred to pretend that they were financing a development project, not covering balance of payments deficits.

With the next president-general, João Figueiredo, Antônio Delfim Netto, the 'father' of the miracle, came back to power. As he had no commitment to the grandiose projects undertaken by the previous administration, he had few scruples in abandoning most of them half-finished, and adopting recessionary measures, somewhat half-heartedly, as a way of reducing demand and increasing export surpluses. But he carried on with the policy of running up excessive debts, raising loans for the most bizarre projects, such as the Proalcool scheme for substituting home-grown sugar-cane fuel for imported oil, a scheme that did not require a single cent's worth of imported equipment. He also negotiated 'financial packages' with the commercial banks, in which cash loans were made conditional on Brazil accepting large amounts of supplier's credit, that is, loans that could be spent only on importing machinery and equipment from the creditor country. This meant that, much to the annoyance of Brazil's new, dynamic capital goods industry, the country was forced to import equipment that could have been produced locally or, worse still, was not even required and was left to rust in warehouses. 'The debt was really a way of paying for the oil. The projects didn't need dollars', Delfim was to admit, years later.[18]

Though they were clearly being used as an instrument for raising much of the foreign finance, the state companies were satisfied, for their financial power increased as they were given in cruzeiros the equivalent, or almost the equivalent, of the foreign loans they raised. For them too, it was the easiest money in the world, making it very difficult for any manager to impose austerity.

At the same time, as the combined result of the world recession, the increase in interest rates and delays or cancellations, many of the big projects undertaken by Geisel did not earn dollars, as some of them should have done, but instead began to eat up enormous amounts of foreign currency in debt servicing. The Itaipu hydroelectric power station, which was planned as a joint venture with Paraguay in 1973, was supposed to have an installed capacity of 12,600 megawatts, at a total cost of $3.6 billion. It would have supplied the cheapest electricity in the world, at $0.056 per kilowatt-hour. Though the project was relatively well administered, the construction costs had risen, ten years later, to $5.6 billion. At the same time, as a result of the exorbitant interest rates on the world financial market, it was forced to pay each year an extra $500 million on the huge loans it had contracted at floating interest rates. As the management could make these payments only by additional borrowing, the total cost of the project was pushed up to about three times the original figure. The feasibility study had expected interest rates to be 10 per cent throughout the time of construction — but in fact, for a period, they reached 20 per cent. The Açominas steel mill was planned to cost $3.4 billion, including $218 million in interest, and to be producing 4 million tonnes of steel by 1980; by 1986, $5.7 billion, including $2.3 billion in interest, had been spent on it, though its capacity had been cut to half the original figure. The nuclear programme, based on doubtful technology and with ambiguous targets, was an almost unmitigated disaster.

The chickens came home to roost earlier in Brazil than in most other Latin American countries, because, as an oil importer, it was subjected to an extra burden. Though Brazil did not go broke until late 1982, after Mexico, debt servicing was absorbing 86 per cent of new borrowing by as early as 1979, and Brazil was sending abroad more hard currency than it was receiving. Between the end of 1976 and the end of 1981, Brazil received $73.9 billion in foreign loans, but spent 75 per cent — $55.8 billion — on debt-servicing, and lost another $7.1 billion in capital flight. The country received a net transfer of just $5.0 billion during the five-year period. It is remarkable how the whole debt crisis was provoked by such a tiny influx of resources.

Chile: the Chicago Boys

In Chile, a group of economists known as the Chicago Boys (because many of them had studied at Chicago University) came to power with General Augusto Pinochet. As in Brazil, these economists had gained little credibility under the earlier civilian regimes, which had favoured Keynesian-style policies. Espousing highly conservative political doctrines, most of them had few scruples in working with an authoritarian government and, in fact, favoured a military – technocratic alliance that could rule without adapting its policies to the demands of politicians.

Many of the Chicago Boys had close personal links with key monetarist figures in the industrialised countries, such as Friedrich Von Hayek, Milton Friedman and Arnold Harbeger. These economists also had a big impact on the new monetarist counter-revolution being carried out in the USA by Reagan and Volcker and in Britain by Margaret Thatcher (who is said to have been greatly impressed by Hayek's *The Road to Serfdom*, a virulent attack on Keynesianism).

Chicago taught these economists to put their faith in market forces and to lift as far as possible all restrictions that might interfere with them. Friedman firmly rejected any suggestion that Chile's economic difficulties might be caused by the convulsions on the world market caused by Reagan's policies and the oil shocks. 'No', he said on a visit, 'Chile's problems are manufactured in this country'. They would be resolved, he explained, by 'shock treatment that will amputate the diseased limb' (the state sector) and open the economy to the cold but invigorating winds of world competition.[19]

The shock treatment, called the Economic Recovery Programme, was announced in April 1975, after virtually no discussion within the government. Public expenditure was cut drastically, state companies privatised, the Chilean peso devalued and, with a few exceptions, import tariffs reduced to a uniform 10 per cent. By 1980, only 15 of a previous total of 507 public companies were still state-run.[20]

The social cost was enormous, far greater than the Chicago Boys had predicted. Gross domestic product fell 16.6 per cent in 1975, perhaps a world record outside times of war.[21] Manufacturing was hurt more than any other sector, with some industries completely wiped out. Wages, left to find their 'market level', had fallen by 1975 to 47.9 per cent of their 1970 level. By the beginning of 1976, unemployment officially stood at 19.8 per cent, or a remarkable 28 per cent if the people working on emergency programmes set up by the government are included.

However, in the following year, the economy began to recover, growing 5 per cent in 1976 and 8.6 per cent in 1977, apparently justifying the monetarists' policies. Export products in which Chile had a natural comparative advantage, such as some minerals, timber and seafood, did well, and Chile became a monetarist show-case. Arnold Harbeger visited Chile again to bask in the adoration of his disciples. He declared solemnly: 'One can predict that in ten years Chileans will enjoy a standard of living similar to that of Spain, which today has a domestic product about double Chile's. In 20 years time, they will probably have the same standard of living as the Dutch.'[22]

But it was a fool's paradise, based on the enormous idle capacity created by the 1975 recession. The rate of gross fixed capital investment, which had been around 20 per cent of GDP in the 1960s, fell to 15.5 per cent between 1974 and 1982.[23] Industry, rather than developing under monetarism, took a big step backwards. 'Our textile industry used to produce what we proudly called English cloth', commented one politician. 'You could get as good a suit in Chile as anywhere in London. But now the industry is in ruins and everything is imported.'[24]

Table 8.3
Chile: the flow of resources
($ bn)

	1977	78	79	80	81	82	83	84	85	86
Outflow										
Net services (total)(a)	0.7	0.8	0.9	1.3	2.2	2.3	2.2	2.4	2.2	2.3
interest	0.3	0.4	0.6	0.9	1.5	1.8	1.5	1.8	1.9	1.9
others	0.4	0.4	0.3	0.4	0.7	0.5	0.7	0.6	0.3	0.4
Amortisation*(b)	0.7	1.1	1.3	1.4	1.8	1.2	0.9	0.4	0.4	0.4
Other outflows**(c)	-0.5	-0.5	-0.2	-0.5	-0.1	1.2	-0.3	-0.4	-0.4	-0.7
Total (d=a+b+c)	0.9	1.4	2.0	2.2	3.9	4.7	2.8	2.4	2.2	2.0
Inflow										
Loans (e)	1.0	2.3	3.2	4.1	6.2	2.9	1.2	2.1	1.2	0.7
Foreign investment(f)	0.0	0.2	0.2	0.2	0.4	0.3	0.1	0.0	0.1	0.2
Total (g=e+f)	1.0	2.5	3.4	4.3	6.6	3.2	1.3	2.1	1.3	0.9
Net Transfer										
(h=g-d)	**0.1**	**1.1**	**1.4**	**2.1**	**2.7**	**-1.5**	**-1.5**	**-0.3**	**-0.9**	**-1.1**
(h=i+j)										
Achieved through:										
Trade balance***(i)	0.0	0.4	0.3	0.8	2.6	-0.2	-1.0	-0.3	-0.8	-1.1
Net change in reserves****(j)	0.1	0.7	1.1	1.3	0.1	-1.3	-0.5	0.0	-0.1	0.0

*   It covers amortisation of all long and medium-term debt.
**   This figure is residual and is calculated according to the methodology described in Table 2.1.
***   A trade surplus is represented by a minus sign as it indicates a flow of resources out of the region.
****   A decrease in reserves is indicated by a minus sign, as it indicates a flow of resources out of the region.

Sources: 1. IDB annual reports; 2. ECLAC annual reports; 3. World Debt Tables, World Bank; 4. Calculated from ECLAC's annual figures for gross foreign debt and the World Bank's amortisation figures

The authors of this shock treatment had hoped that it would attract heavy foreign investment that would turn Chile into a South Korea or a Taiwan, and, indeed, deliberately sought to keep interest rates high to attract foreigners. Foreign resources, indeed, came flooding in — at its peak, about $3 million was coming in each day — but almost all of it was in the form of loans, with foreign banks lending to Chilean banks which then re-lent the money to the private sector, which, deprived of local funds because of the drastic reduction in lending by the state banks, was pleased to borrow under almost any conditions. The profits for the Chilean banks were enormous; they would borrow abroad at 12 per cent, then pass the money on at 35−40 per cent.

Corruption was rife. Despite central bank restrictions, banks lent to companies within the same group, who did not invest the money in production, as the interest was too high to make this viable. Instead, they used the money to speculate in property and to buy up state companies sold at knock-down prices as part of the government's privatisation programme. There is little doubt that without the heavy influx of foreign capital the much-vaunted privatisation programme would have failed. And, as this programme led to a significant strengthening of big economic groups,[25] foreign loans can be said to have contributed to yet a further concentration of income in Chile.

The Javier Vial group alone, which owned the Banco Hipotecario de Chile, the Banco de Chile and numerous other companies, borrowed half a billion dollars. Neither this group nor the other big conglomerate — Cruzat-Larrain, which owned the Banco de Santiago and about 200 other companies — had existed in 1960. Both had close links with the Chicago Boys and had grown very fast. They became known as the 'piranhas'.

The government did little to eliminate the abuses, because they believed that regulations were a hindrance to economic development. 'They never enforced credit regulations with any enthusiasm, because they thought the "invisible hand" of the market-place would be sufficient', commented Alfredo Moreno Charme, an economics lecturer; 'They sincerely believed in market forces'.

Years later, former finance minister Rolf Luders and former bank superintendent Boris Blanco were charged with fraud in connection with loans above the legal limit made to the Vial group though the Banco Andino, a bank that was set up in Panama apparently for this purpose. The opportunities for profit from speculation were enormous. It is believed that, unlike the rest of Latin America, which was indulging in capital flight out of the continent, Chile was a net receiver of 'hot money' between 1977 and 1981. Faith in the Chicago Boys was so great that many foreign banks did not initially demand government guarantees, as they did in most of Latin America.

The gross influx of foreign capital was $4.3 billion in 1980 and $6.6 billion in 1981 (*see* Table 8.3), equivalent to 23 and 30 per cent, respectively, of GDP, compared with a maximum of 9 per cent in Brazil and 21 per cent in Mexico. Chile's debt with the commercial banks rose from $5.4 billion in 1976 to $15.7 billion in 1981, one of the fastest increases in the world, making Chile the fifth largest debtor to the commercial banks by 1981. The influx was so heavy that, despite repeated trade deficits, Chile was able to build up large foreign reserves.

But Chile became so dependent on these foreign resources that, when the crisis finally erupted in 1982, the country was hit with particular force. By then the foreign debt was $17.1 billion, equivalent to 90 per cent of its GDP, one of the highest ratios in Latin America. When it became evident early in 1982 that collapse was imminent, the same bankers and speculators who had brought in dollars in the 1970s began to take them out. For six months, the Chicago Boys stubbornly refused to admit that their 'free market' policies were not only ineffective but actually feeding the crisis. By July, about $1.3 billion had fled the country.

Eventually, and with great reluctance, the government began to act, though its first measure was aimed solely at protecting the interests of the creditor banks. On 12 July 1982, the Central Bank took over the so-called 'carteras vencidas', or the local banks' bad debts, worth about $1.5 billion. If it had not done this, there would have been a spate of bankruptcies and Chile would have been forced to default on its debt. In August, when about $2 billion had left the country and the foreign reserves were falling at an alarming rate, the finance minister finally allowed the peso to float freely against the dollar. It was a tacit recognition that his policies had failed, for according to strict monetarist theory the government's free market policies should have made it impossible for the peso to become overvalued. The dollar immediately shot up from 47 pesos to about 60.

In typically brusque fashion, President Pinochet not only ignored the contradiction inherent in the measure, but welcomed it as the solution. 'Over the last fortnight, they've got out $300 million, but they won't get any more', he said.[26] Brave words, but the outflow was not easy to stem, particularly for a government that would not contemplate exchange controls. The demand for dollars continued, pushing the exchange rate up to 70 pesos. To try to reduce demand, the government sold more and more dollars. Its reserves fell by $1.3 billion, the size of the record increase in 1980.

The turnround in the balance of payments was extremely abrupt. After receiving a net influx of $2.7 billion in 1981, Chile made a net transfer to foreign banks outside the country of $1.5 billion in 1982. In a single year, Chile was deprived of $4.2 billion, equivalent to about one-fifth of its economic output. It was scarcely surprising that GDP fell by 14.3 per cent and manufacturing output by 21.6 per cent. It was the most violent recession in the continent.

Despite the government's efforts to bail it out, Chile's banking system began to collapse. Later investigations showed that the country's leading banks had borrowed four times the value of their capital and reserves and were responsible for one-sixth of Chile's debt. General Pinochet had made his own personal contribution to the squandering: he had spent $18 million on a six-storey mansion, equipped with a private cinema, a gymnasium, saunas, and kitchens able to cater for 2,000 people.[27]

But although ordinary people had been excluded from the spending spree, they were left with the bill. The Chicago Boys, who eight years earlier had privatised the financial system, now nationalised its debts. As we shall see later, the Pinochet government was responsible for one of the most outrageous episodes in the whole Latin American debt scandal, taking over responsibility for private sector debts in return for absolutely nothing from the foreign banks.

Argentina: dirty war and capital flight

Argentina's monetarist phase began more than a year later than Chile's, after the military coup of March 1976, which overthrew María Estela de Perón. Unlike Brazil, which was suffering from the oil shock, and Mexico, which squandered its oil earnings, Argentina systematically obtained trade surpluses throughout this period, as a result of the longest and deepest recession in its history.

In contrast to the Chilean experience, which, in extraordinary fashion, created a new privileged social group almost from nothing, Argentine monetarism furthered the interests of a powerful, established socio-economic elite. To this extent, the Argentine monetarists were more pragmatic and less concerned with ideological purity than their Chilean counterparts.

On two previous occasions — 1959–1961, during the presidency of the civilian Arturo Frondizi, with Alvaro Alsogaray as finance minister, and 1967–1968, during the presidency of General Juan Carlos Ongania, with Krieger Vasena as finance minister — the same group had attempted to attract international capital. On both occasions, all controls over capital movements were lifted and the exchange rate for financial operations was fixed. Huge profits were to be made, for Argentina's real interest rate was 20 per cent a year, compared with 4 per cent on the world market, but little capital was drawn in. It seems that the international banks were not yet ready.

In 1976, Martínez de Hoz, the new economic tsar brought in by the military after they had overthrown María Estela de Perón, made another attempt. Following the example of his friend Krieger Vasena, he established two exchange rates: one fixed, for financial operations; one floating, for trade. During this period, the dual exchange rate was essential, for, with inflation already over 100 per cent, Argentina's exports would have rapidly lost their competitive edge if the exchange rate had been fixed throughout the economy.

The set-up was tempting for foreign investors. Dollars could be brought into the country, converted into pesos and invested in government bonds, indexed for inflation. At the end of the year, the bonds could be redeemed for a much larger sum of pesos and changed back into dollars. It has been calculated[28] that $100, invested in April 1976 for one year, yielded $250 — an impressive return of 150 per cent, with no risk. But even with this succulent profit, the scheme attracted only $500 million, partly because it was uncertain whether Martínez de Hoz would survive as finance minister, and partly because there was not yet excessive liquidity on the world financial market.

However, as Martínez de Hoz strengthened his position, particularly after General Jorge Videla accepted another three-year term of office, and as world liquidity increased, the influx of dollars grew. At the end of 1978, Martínez de Hoz lifted almost all the remaining trade barriers and, with inflation now falling, introduced a single exchange rate. By now, his policies were very similar to those introduced by the Chicago Boys in Chile — indeed, it is now known that Chileans were advising the Argentines at this time.

The influx reached $4.7 billion in 1979, though the rate of return dropped significantly, to 34 per cent in real terms. Almost all of it went to a small, privileged group of businessmen and transnational subsidiaries that were well-placed to take advantage of changes in financial policy. It has been estimated that just 30 companies and a dozen banks were responsible for about half of the private sector's total debt.

The dollars were deposited with the central bank in exchange for pesos. By the end of 1979, the government's foreign reserves had reached $10.5 billion, over half the gross foreign debt ($19.0 billion) and more than the value of the whole of the public sector debt ($10.0 billion). This policy was economic nonsense. Argentina did not need high reserves to cover a trade deficit. And the reserves earned substantially less interest than the country was paying on its foreign loans.

As in Chile, the monetarists' exchange and financial policies had a very harmful effect on the local economy. The overvalued peso made imports very cheap, while it became almost impossible to sell Argentine manufactured goods abroad. Argentina, which traditionally had had one of the healthiest foreign accounts in Latin America, began to have to borrow abroad to cover its deficit. The seeds of a balance of payments crisis, similar to the one experienced in the rest of Latin America, had been planted.

The monetarist experiment in Argentina lasted for a much shorter period than it did in Chile. In 1980, it began to crumble, not as a result of external factors, which was eventually the case in Chile, but because of the instability of the military regime, which was far less stable than General Pinochet's.

Many of the banks had borrowed heavily abroad and passed the loans on to local manufacturers. But these manufacturers soon began to face problems. Because of the lifting of import controls, imported goods flooded the market, being sold at prices with which the local manufacturers, with higher production costs, simply could not compete. With a flurry of bankruptcies in the manufacturing sector, the banks soon found that many of the foreign debts were not being serviced. By as early as March 1980, the government had had to take over three private banks that had accumulated heavy arrears in foreign debt payments.

By the end of the year, with General Roberto Viola now nominated as the next president, to take over in March 1981, Argentina had an unprecedented trade deficit of $2.5 billion (*see* Table 8.4), created largely by a flood of cheap imported goods. The government began to face a serious crisis of confidence. Rumours were rife that, to deal with the deteriorating balance of payments, General Viola's new economic team would have to introduce far-reaching changes, including a maxi-devaluation.

Private groups began to buy dollars from the government, both as speculation and as a guarantee for their earlier foreign loans, which they were still servicing in dollars. The Argentine economy began to spew out dollars as rapidly as it had sucked them in during the previous year. Central bank reserves fell by $6.2 billion between the end of December 1979 and the end of March 1981. During the same period, the government borrowed another $7.2 billion from abroad. In just 15 months, the Argentine public sector went from being a creditor, with a surplus of $500m, to a debtor, owing abroad $12.9 billion. As the private sector had borrowed $3.3 billion during this period, the Argentine net foreign debt (that is, its gross foreign debt minus reserves) went from $8.5 billion to $25.3 billion during the same year and a quarter. It was probably the most rapid increase recorded by any country in the whole history of the debt crisis.

What actually happened was a rapid transfer of resources from the public sector to the private. The government ran down its reserves and borrowed more dollars, so that a small group of Argentine and transnational companies could build up huge dollar deposits abroad. It has been calculated that 60 per cent of the money borrowed during the first quarter of 1981, that is, about $10.1 billion, fled the country. The money, in fact, made a full circle, a procedure that in Argentina was aptly called the 'bicycle': it was lent by the commercial banks to the Argentine public sector, which sold it to private groups, who then deposited it abroad with the commercial banks. It was an outrageous process masquerading behind the monetarists' deference to the 'free market', saddling the public sector with a huge foreign debt, while allowing a few private groups to obtain large and lucrative dollar deposits abroad.

Table 8.4
Argentina: the flow of resources
($ bn)

	1977	78	79	80	81	82	83	84	85	86
Outflow										
Net services (total)(a)	0.8	1.1	2.4	3.4	5.4	4.9	6.4	6.4	5.6	5.2
interest	0.5	0.7	1.2	2.2	3.4	3.8	5.5	5.3	5.3	4.4
others	0.3	0.4	1.2	1.2	2.0	1.1	0.9	1.1	0.3	0.8
Amortisation*(b)	0.7	1.6	0.9	1.2	1.1	1.0	1.0	1.0	1.0	2.0
Other outflows**(c)	0.3	2.4	1.3	5.5	7.7	6.5	0.2	0.8	2.2	1.2
Total (d=a+b+c)	1.8	5.1	4.6	10.1	14.2	12.4	7.6	8.2	8.8	8.4
Inflow										
Loans(e)	2.1	4.4	7.4	9.2	9.6	8.9	1.2	4.7	2.4	3.2
Foreign investment(f)	0.1	0.3	0.3	0.8	0.9	0.2	0.2	0.2	1.0	0.6
Total (g=e + f)	2.2	4.7	7.7	10.0	10.5	9.1	1.4	1.4	3.4	3.8
Net Transfer										
(h=g−d)	0.4	−0.4	3.1	−0.1	−3.7	−3.3	−6.2	−3.3	−5.4	−4.6
(h = i + j)										
Achieved through:										
Trade balance***(i)	−1.4	−2.6	−1.1	2.5	−0.7	−2.7	−3.7	−3.9	−4.9	−2.5
Net change in reserves****(j)	1.8	2.2	4.2	−2.6	−3.0	−0.6	−2.5	−0.6	−0.5	−2.1

* It covers amortisation of all long- and medium-term debt.
** This figure is residual and is calculated according to the methodology described in Table 2.1.
*** A trade surplus is represented by a minus sign as it indicates a flow of resources out of the region.
**** A decrease in reserves is indicated by a minus sign, as it indicates a flow of resources out of the region.

Sources: 1. IDB annual reports; 2. ECLAC annual reports; 3. World Debt Tables, World Bank; 4. Calculated from ECLAC's annual figures for gross foreign debt and the World Bank's amortisation figures

The current account in the balance of payments recorded a rapid deterioration, deliberately provoked by the monetarists. After a surplus of $1.9 billion in 1978, this account ran increasingly large deficits: $500m in 1979 and an enormous $1.9 billion in 1980. As foreign exchange controls were anathema to them, the monetarists could only sit out the storm and cover the deficit with additional borrowing until what they saw as the country's 'truly competitive sectors' emerged. Our table (8.4) reveals the full extent of the crisis. Between the end of 1976 and the end of 1980, Argentina received a gross influx of foreign loans of $23.1 billion, of which $9.0 billion was used in debt-servicing and another $9.5 billion left the country as 'other outflows', largely capital flight. Argentina is the only one of the big debtors in which, during the build-up to the crisis, capital flight probably absorbed more resources than debt-servicing. During this period, Argentina received a small net transfer of resources, of $3 billion. The crisis hit Argentina before it hit the other debtor nations, because of the sudden collapse in local investors' confidence in the government. In 1981, while the rest of Latin America was still receiving more dollars than it was sending abroad, Argentina was already exporting capital, to the tune of $3.7 billion. This was not due to any reluctance in the creditor banks to lend, for borrowing ran at a record level — $9.6 billion. Rather, it was the result of high interest payments ($3.4 billion) and, even more, of remarkable capital flight (possibly as much as $7.7 billion).

With small local variations, the ingredients that led to the snowballing foreign debts in Brazil, Argentina, Chile and Mexico, were found in the other countries of the continent. Despite considerable political differences between the nations, the figures are depressingly similar.

Overall, Latin America borrowed $272.9 billion between the end of 1976 and the end of 1981 (*see* Table 2.1, page 16.) Of this, 21 per cent, or $56.6 billion, left the continent without a specific destination ('other capital movements'), most of which was probably capital flight. Another $22.9 billion, or 8.9 per cent of the total, was used to build up foreign reserves in an attempt to gain some kind of protection from balance of payments crises. But by far the biggest sum — $170.5 billion, or 62 per cent of the total — went on amortisation and interest payments. The amount spent on debt-servicing had risen steadily, from $17.8 billion in 1977, to $25.6 billion in 1978, to $37.4 billion in 1979, to $39.8 billion in 1980 and $49.9 billion in 1981. The foreign debt had become a huge monster requiring more and more loans to satisfy its appetite.

These three items — capital flight, foreign reserves and debt-servicing — accounted for $250 billion, 91.6 per cent of the total. None of this expenditure made any contribution to regional development. Only a tiny amount — $22.9 billion, or 8.4 percent of the total — was used for investment.

To some extent, this interpretation seems to conflict with empirical evidence, for many of the debtor nations, particularly Brazil, Mexico and Venezuela, invested heavily in development projects during this period. The answer is that the projects were set up with great pomp and ceremony, to be paraded in front of the foreign bankers, who liked to believe that they were funding 'development'. But, once the loan was in the bag, the project was either abandoned or developed largely with local funding. Such development as did occur — and it was considerable in some countries — could have been undertaken without the foreign loans if the local banking system had been expanded to handle it. Most development projects, be they the construction of a national highway, the building of a steel mill, or the setting up of a big farming scheme, require a much heavier outlay in local currency than in dollars. In any case, if most of the foreign borrowing had gone into development, it would have been reflected in the trade balance, as the only real contribution that the foreign currency could have made to development would have been through increased imports. Yet, from the end of 1976 to the end of 1981, Latin America ran an accumulated trade deficit of only $2.7 billion which, if higher than its historical average, was negligible compared with the influx of foreign resources.

While the foreign funding made only a small positive contribution to regional development, it exercised a significant pernicious influence — exactly the opposite of the claims of the Latin American governments, and the opposite of what happened during the years soon after the Second World War with loans from the IDB and the World Bank. In their craving for foreign loans, Latin American governments often assembled development projects in great haste. Their chief concern was not to make the best use of limited resources, but to put together a project that would impress bankers. All too often, this meant a grandiose mega-project which, even if it had gone ahead as planned, would have produced few benefits for the local population and, very often, considerable harm to the environment.

Moreover, the creditor banks often made their loans conditional on the purchase of foreign equipment for the project they were officially funding. Huge financial packages were constructed, in which part of the finance was a normal commercial loan, but the rest came in the form of supplier's credit, that is, tied to the purchase of equipment produced in the country providing the loan. In other words, the banks not only insisted on high spreads that provided fat profits, but also won orders for capital goods produced in their own countries by manufacturers who were, at that time, suffering from serious problems of idle capacity.

Notes

1. Robert Pringle, *The Banker*, February 1974.
2. Anthony Sampson, *The Money Lenders*, Hodder & Stoughton, 1981.
3. Ibid.
4. 'Latin American debt hangs in the balance', *NACLA Report*, vol. 19, no. 2, March–April 1985.
5. Anthony Sampson, op.cit.
6. Quoted in John Wells, *Estudos Cebrap*, no. 6.
7. 'Debt remains a problem', *Foreign Policy*, Spring 1978, Washington, USA.
8. Robert Devlin, 'Renegotiation of Latin American Debt', *Cepal Review*, no. 20, August 1983.
9. *Financial Times*, 1978.
10. John Rettie, *Guardian*, 4 August 1982.
11. Ibid.
12. See Sérgio Goldstein, *A Dívida Externa Brasileira*, ed. Guanabara, 1986; and Paulo Davidoff Cruz, *Dívida Externa e Política Econômica*, Brasiliense, 1984.
13. Planning ministry study, quoted in *Jornal do Brasil*, 30 May 1976, p.40.
14. See Goldstein and Davidoff, op. cit.
15. Our estimate.
16. John Wells, op.cit.

17. Carlos Alberto Monteiro, *Revista de Saude Publica*, no. 16, 1982.
18. Interview with *Correio Braziliense*, 7 May 1986, p. 13.
19. *Chile: The Pinochet Decade*, Latin America Bureau, London, 1983.
20. *Guardian*, 16 November 1984.
21. *Chile: The Pinochet Decade*, p.63
22. Richard Gott, *Guardian*, 15 March 1983.
23. Ricardo Ffrench-Davis, 'La crisis de la deuda externa en Chile: una sintesis', mimeographed paper, conference on Latin American debt at UNICAMP University, Campinas, Brazil, 1985.
24. *International Herald Tribune*, 21 September 1983.
25. Ricardo Ffrench-Davis, op. cit.
26. *Latin America Weekly Report*, 13 August 1986.
27. *Guardian*, 16 November 1984.
28. *Sunday Times*, 6 May 1984.

9. Reaganomics Against Latin America

How the adoption by President Ronald Reagan of a new conservative economic doctrine led to the final collapse of Latin America

Basic approaches demand time, and we have already wasted a lot of time. But fortunately we start from a position of strength. I am sure that we will take full advantage of the opportunities in front of us.

Paul Volcker, chairman of the Fed, in his testimony to the foreign affairs committee in the US Senate, quoted in *O Estado de S. Paulo*, 9 June 1985.

It was in 1979 that the final tug was given, a tug that three years later was to pull the carpet completely from under Latin America. On 6 October 1979, Paul Volcker, chairman of the Fed, radically changed the way of controlling the money supply in the US. He decided on such a severe monetary squeeze that prime rate jumped from 9 per cent to 12, then to 16, reaching 20 per cent in May 1980. In January 1981 it reached the all-time record of 21.5 per cent, 'the highest interest rate since the birth of Jesus Christ', in the words of the West German Chancellor, Helmut Schmidt. Libor, the rate applied to another large part of Latin America's debt, rose with prime; it did not quite reach the same dizzy level, but peaked at 18 per cent (*see* Figure 9.1).

Trapped by floating interest rates, Latin America had to pay an extra $1.8 billion for every increase of one percentage point. In just three years — 1981, 1982 and 1983 — Latin America forked out $94.8 billion in interest payments, twice its total outlay on interest for the whole of the 1970s. Mexico's interest bill tripled, from $2.3 billion in 1979 to $36.1 billion in 1982, and it was the first country to go under. It was soon followed by Brazil, whose interest bill increased two and a half times, reaching $11.9 billion in 1982. For the region as a whole, interest payments more than doubled, from $14.4 billion in 1979 to $36.1 billion in 1982.

Reaganomics

This new monetary policy, which together with Reagan's fiscal policies became known as Reaganomics, lasted until 1985. During these six years Latin America paid $181 billion in interest, but even this was not enough. Latin America had to borrow heavily to cover the shortfall and its debt doubled to $377 billion. During the whole history of capitalism, there is no other case of such intense income appropriation by strictly banking methods. According to the meticulous calculations made by Keynes, the harsh war reparations imposed on Germany by the Treaty of Versailles, which plundered the country of most of its wealth and paved the way for Nazism and the Second World War, were worth between £6.4 billion and £8 billion, which is equivalent to $250 billion in 1985 currency.[1]

If we calculate just the excess interest paid by Latin America, comparing the

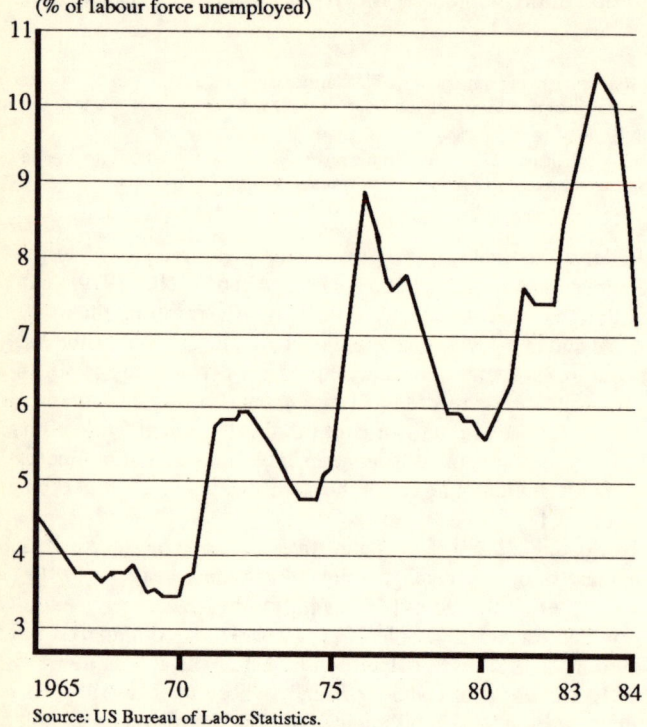

Figure 9.1

Growing Unemployment in the US

(% of labour force unemployed)

Source: US Bureau of Labor Statistics.

rates under Reaganomics with traditional rates, we also reach remarkable results. After taking inflation into account by subtracting from prime the rate of increase in the US consumer price index, Stephen Kanitz worked out that, during the 15 years before Reaganomics, the average rate of real interest on the international financial market was about 1 per cent.[2] If we consider this to be a just rate of return for financial capital, we can work out the excess interest paid by Latin America by adding this 1 per cent to the rate of dollar inflation and then comparing this total with the interest effectively paid by Latin America. These calculations suggest that excess interest payments totalled $93.9 billion during the six years of Reaganomics, or $103 billion if we include the two previous years, when interest rates were already rising (*see* Table 9.1). By the same criteria, Brazil alone paid $30.2 billion in excess interest rates during the six-year period, or $33 billion if the two additional years are included (*see* Table 9.2).

Other writers have reached similar conclusions by other routes. Ernane Galvêas,

Table 9.1
The extortionate interest paid by Latin America
(Excess interest in relation to the historic rate of 1%)

	(A) Interest paid ($ bn)	(B) Accumulated Interest paid ($ bn)	(C) Libor (%)	(D) Excessive Interest (%)	(E) Annual Excess Paid ($ m)	(F) Accumulated Excess Paid ($ m)	(G) Factor	(H) Gross Foreign Debt ($ bn)
1973	2.9*	2.9	—	—	—	—	—	—
1974	3.5*	6.4	10.2	2.4	686	686		
1975	3.8*	10.2	6.6	−1.7	−748	−62	−0.197	68.5
1976	4.8*	15.0	5.4	1.2	777	715	0.162	89.4
1977	6.1	21.1	7.5	2.7	2,196	2,911	0.36	107.2
1978	8.2	29.3	12.3	5.9	3,362	6,273	0.41	133.7
1979	14.4	43.7	14.4	6.8	5,904	12,177	0.41	182.0
1980	18.3	62.0	16.4	8.2	8,052	20,229	0.44	222.5
1981	27.3	89.3	14.9	6.3	11,739	31,968	0.43	277.8
1982	36.1	125.4	9.5	4.5	14,079	46,047	0.39	318.4
1983	31.4	156.8	10.2	7.4	18,840	64,887	0.60	344.0
1984	34.8	191.6	11.2	8.5	22,272	87,159	0.64	366.5
1985	33.1	224.7	9.0	6.3	18,867	106,026	0.57	376.6

(A) Effective net disbursement of interest, according to ECLAC.
(B) Accumulated disbursement.
(C) Average LIBOR for 180 days
(D) LIBOR plus 2 per cent of spread and commissions, minus 1 per cent of 'just' remuneration, minus world inflation.
(E) Excess interest calculated by the following formula (A × D/C +2).
(F) Accumulated excess.
(G) Multiplication factor = D/LIBOR + 2, which multiplied by the interest effectively paid (A), determines the proportion of this interest which is excessive.
(H) Gross foreign debt at year-end.

Brazil's finance minister when a considerable part of the debt was contracted, presented figures during a speech to the Higher War College which suggested that, between 1974 and 1984, Brazil lost $30.9 billion through excess interest payments.[3] In fact, Galvêas's calculations were not accurate, as he did not even subtract from the gross foreign debt the country's international reserves that were benefiting from the higher interest rates. His intention was probably to make an impression on foreign bankers on the eve of yet another round of debt rescheduling talks. More careful calculations have been made by other economists. Albert Fishlow put at $20 billion the losses made by the whole of the developing world through high interest rates in just two years of Reaganomics (1981 and 1982).[4] By including increases in fixed capital costs, not reflected in interest remittances, Philippe Collier from the Royal Bank of Canada estimated their losses during these same two years at $22 billion.[5] William Cline reached a figure of $44.5 billion for the same period.[6] Though they are all substantial, the estimates vary considerably, largely as a result of the methodological difficulty of calculating 'real' interest, in a period of great volatility in both nominal interest rates and inflation.

These were only the direct losses. Albert Fishlow has calculated that the recession in 1981 and 1982 cost the periphery countries another $59.4 billion through

Table 9.2

The extortionate interest paid by Brazil

(The excess interest, in relation to the historic average of 1%)

	(A) Interest Paid ($ m)	(B) Accumulated Interest Paid ($ m)	(C) Libor (%)	(D) Excessive Interest (%)	(E) Annual Excess paid ($ m)	(F) Accumulated Excess Paid ($ m)
1973	514	—	—	—	—	—
1974	625	1,139	10.2	2.4	122	122
1975	1,498	2,637	6.6	−1.7	−296	−174
1976	1,810	4,437	5.4	1.2	293	119
1977	2,103	6,550	7.5	2.7	597	716
1978	2,696	9,246	12.3	5.9	1,112	1,828
1979	4,186	13,432	14.4	6.8	1,735	3,563
1980	6,311	19,743	16.4	8.2	2,812	6,375
1981	9,161	28,904	14.9	6.3	3,415	9,790
1982	11,358	40,262	9.5	4.5	4,444	14,234
1983	9,555	49,817	10.2	7.4	5,795	20,029
1984	10,400	60,217	11.2	8.5	6,696	26,725
1985	12,350	72,567	9.0	6.3	7,073	33,798

(A) is the effective net disbursement of interest (interest paid minus interest received), according to the Central Bank of Brazil.
(B) is the accumulated disbursement.
(C) Average LIBOR for 180 days.
(D) LIBOR plus 2 per cent of spread and commissions minus the 1 per cent remuneration considered 'just', minus world inflation.
(E) Excess interest calculated by applying the formula $(A \times D/C + 2)$.
(F) Total of excess.

the fall in both the volume and the price of their exported goods. It was even more than the loss they incurred, estimated by Fishlow at $55.4 billion, as a result of the second oil shock, which took place at the same time. IMF calculations show that, during the severe recession from 1979 to 1982, the price of agricultural raw materials and metals fell, respectively, by 20 and 25 per cent.[7] William Cline put at $78.6 billion the losses to the developing world as a result of the decline in the volume and the price of world trade. Collier, on the other hand, estimated this loss at $36 billion.

Because of considerable differences in methodology, the overall figures, reached by the various writers, for total loss suffered by the developing countries during just two years of Reaganomics vary widely, but they are all high: $58 billion by Collier, $123 billion by Cline and $133 billion by Fishlow. None of these estimates includes the localised but heavy losses caused by bankrupt companies or the halting of new projects, abandoned half-way as a result of the recession or the extraordinarily high interest rates.

Perhaps there is no one better qualified to explain the negative impact of high interest rates than Jacques de Larosière, managing director of the IMF. Speaking to an audience of bankers in Philadelphia at the end of 1982, three months after the collapse of Mexico, de Larosière said: 'As well as their impact on the servicing of the debt, interest rates are crucial for the debt question because they affect the profitability of projects financed by foreign borrowing, projects that should be generating resources to pay off the debt.'[8] He developed his argument by showing that, worse even than the rise in nominal interest rates was the six-fold increase in real interest rates, that had occurred when inflation had fallen but interest rates had not gone down with it. 'In real terms, that is, adjusting the rates in line with US inflation, the change in real interest rates was even more dramatic [than the change in nominal ones], from 0.9 per cent in the 1973−79 period to 5.2 per cent in the 1979−81 period', he said. 'And, as oil-importing developing countries are net borrowers on the international markets, we should not be surprised that this has had a big impact on their foreign accounts.'

It is tempting to accuse Paul Volcker of intentionally turning Latin America insolvent, so that it could be constantly drained of a substantial part of its income. It is certainly true that Volcker kept a close eye on the snowballing of Latin America's debts and must have known that his policies would have a catastrophic impact on Latin America. In his book, *Inside the Fed*, the economist William Melton said that Volcker 'from the early 1970s, with the first oil shock, became seriously concerned about developments on the international debt market.'[9]

It is true that from the early days the US authorities not only knew about the financial situation of each Latin American debtor nation, but knew about it in great detail. This was because they were fearful of a crisis at the other end of the relationship — the big US creditor banks — if some Latin American country halted interest payments. In December 1975 the Fed and the US Congress had signed an agreement to exchange information about US bank loans to foreign countries. And in 1976 the US Currency Comptroller had begun to monitor the 150 most vulnerable banks.

The underlying cause of high interest rates

But we would be making the same mistake as those who see Hitler's ambitions as the cause of the Second World War if we were to blame Volcker personally for the surge in interest rates. It is true that in normal periods of capitalist expansion real interest rates rarely exceed 1 per cent. This is because the return on this capital must, necessarily, be less than the profit on the investment made with this capital.[10] If this were not the case, no one would want to invest in production. But in periods of acute capitalist crisis this logic is turned on its head and investment in financial transactions becomes more profitable than investment in production. Just as a fever is indicative of an infection, so to have interest rates higher than the rate of profit, as happened under Reaganomics, is a clear sign that the system is in crisis — even if the centre of the system is suffering relatively little, but managing to transfer almost all of the symptoms of the crisis to the periphery.

According to the economist Jay Forrester, high real interest rates are peculiar to periods of sharp depression under capitalism. During the 1930−34 crisis, they reached 12 per cent in real terms, that is, after inflation had been deducted. 'The reason for this is deeply entrenched in the economy and is not a consequence of the Reagan administration or of Paul Volcker of the Fed. It is part of the internal

Figure 9.2
World Interest Rates: Libor for six-month loans
(%)

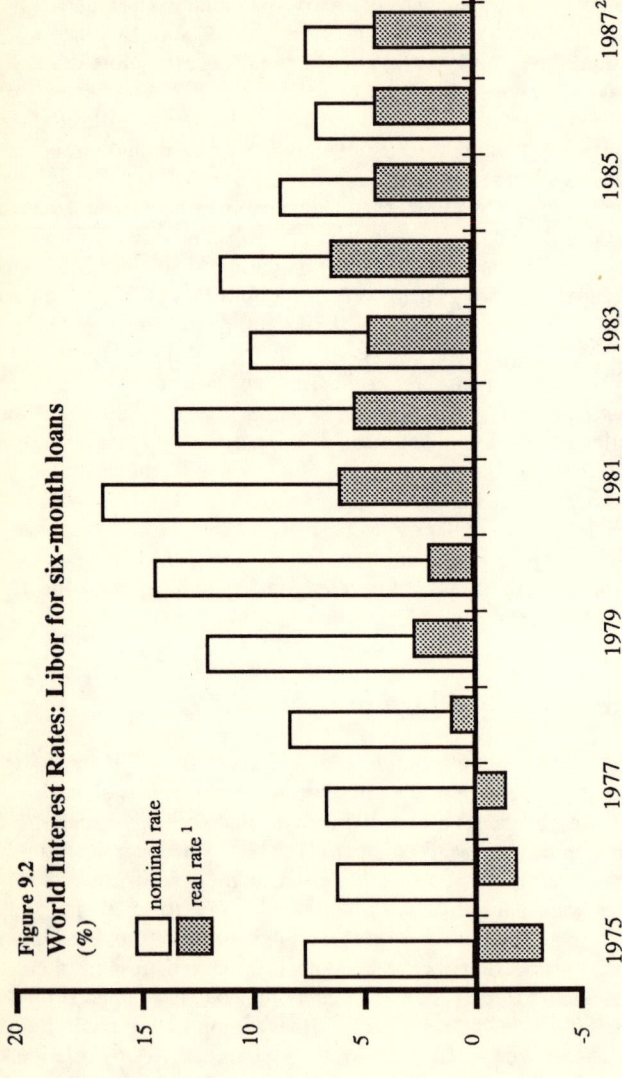

1. Nominal rates deflated by the consumer price index of the industrialised countries.
2. Average January-November.
Source: ECLAC, based on IMF, *International Financial Statistics*.

dynamics of the economic long wave and is what happens to the balance of money, prices and inflation rates as one moves past the peak of the economic long wave'.[11] According to the economist Sosa-Rodrigues, Latin America also paid exorbitant interest during the 1822−25 period, right in the middle of another downward phase in the long wave.[12]

Paul Volcker — and, indeed, the whole Reagan administration — had limited scope for action, for the main economic tendencies had already been established by the downward phase. But this did not mean that they were unable to influence events. By choosing certain policies and not others, they helped determine the form that the crisis assumed. Under their management, the financial hegemony of the dollar took on its most sophisticated form, and it is this that provides the key to understanding the collapse of Latin America.

The oil magnate David Rockefeller, who owns Chase Manhattan Bank, turned down Jimmy Carter's request that he should head the Fed, saying that the American crisis was 'too serious to be handled by a man who was seen as the living symbol of financial capital'.[13] New York bankers then suggested that Carter should ask Paul Volcker, an economist at Rockefeller's bank, who had already worked as an adviser at the Department of the Treasury. Volcker accepted.

The American crisis had indeed reached a highly critical stage. Inflation was rising continuously, reaching double figures and then in 1979 the all-time record of 13.3 per cent. As unemployment was also running at a high level (*see* Figure 9.2), the inflation could not be attributed to the over-heating of the economy. Indeed, economists did not hide their disappointment and perplexity that 'higher and higher inflation was constantly required to obtain the same level of employment', in the words of David P. Calleo. He added: 'The 1960s and 1970s reveal, not so much unfolding strength as accumulating debility. Instead of evolving solutions, there were worsening contradictions.'[14] The same symptoms arose in all the other leading industrialised economies. The average rate of inflation for the seven main countries reached 7.1 per cent in 1979. In West Germany, Great Britain and Japan, unemployment was twice its 1973 level. There were ten million unemployed in Western Europe, seven million in the USA.

The crisis was exacerbated by developments in Iran, where Ayatollah Khomeini, with his fundamentalist Islamic vision, came to power, overthrowing Shah Reza Pahlavi, a key figure in the US military scheme for the Middle East. Immediately oil prices soared to $34 a barrel, wiping out all the efforts by the industrialised countries to balance their current accounts. In 1979, they ran a combined deficit of $39 billion, followed in 1980 by an even larger one, almost double this figure.

The US trade deficit, which had risen to $43 billion in 1982, partly as a result of the violent slump in agricultural commodity prices, made another leap, to $69 billion, in 1983 (*see* Table 9.3). (In 1985, by then as a result of Reaganomics, it was to reach $148 billion.)[15] Just as was to happen yet again in 1987, with the stock market crash and the slide of the dollar on the foreign exchanges, all the symptoms of the first phase of the crisis returned, this time in even more virulent form. As had happened in 1971, the dollar slumped on the foreign exchanges, losing 18 per cent of its value against the other leading currencies. The German Deutschmark and the Japanese yen were the main beneficiaries, increasing 35 and

40 per cent, respectively, against the dollar. David Calleo describes vividly the feeling of imminent disaster that took hold of the financial market at this time:

> The collapsing dollar created near-panic in the exchange markets. The governments of other countries felt at the same time indignant and scared. At the end of the year, the price of gold soared, while the US bond market began to collapse . . . between 10 December and 21 January, the price of gold rose from $431 an ounce to $850 . . . the dramatic collapse of the dollar against gold created fears of a catastrophic end to the dollar as the currency of last reserve and even of the generalised abandonment of paper money.[16]

Paul Volcker, who took on a leadership role in the middle of the crisis, tried to get the Germans to support the dollar, which had fallen to its lowest point, from DM2.60 a dollar to DM1.75. But the Germans, still nursing painful memories of the hyperinflation during the Weimar Republic, insisted, as a condition of their assistance, that measures first be taken to combat US inflation. In New York, the Fed only managed to place treasury bonds at the very high interest rate of 9.8 per cent. And, despite offering a high return, the most powerful US transnational, IBM, failed in its attempt to issue $1 billion in bonds. When Volcker returned from his unsuccessful trip to Bonn, he found the market in a state of near-panic and called an emergency meeting of the main body in the Fed, the Open Market Committee, for the very next day, a Saturday.

Table 9.3
The US financial crisis
($ bn)

	Carter		Reagan I				Reagan II
	1979	1980	1981	1982	1983	1984	1985
Gross domestic product	2,358	2,576	2,886	3,046	3,221	3,581	3,868
Public deficit	40.2	73.8	78.9	127.9	207.8	185.3	222.0
Military budget	116.3	134.0	157.5	185.3	210.0	227.4	254.0
Public deficit/ GDP (%)	1.7	2.8	2.7	4.2	6.4	5.2	5.7
Military budget (%)	25.0	26.0	26.0	30.0	35.0	34.0	34.0
Federal debt	833.0	914.0	1,003.0	1,146.0	1,382.0	1,576.0	1,841.0
Federal debt/ GDP (%)	27.3	27.8	27.5	30.0	35.4	36.6	39.1
Net foreign investment	95.0	105.0	140.0	135.0	96.0	7.0	−100.0
Trade deficit (CIF)	40.4	36.4	36.7	42.7	69.4	123.3	148.4
Current account balance	−1.0	1.9	6.3	−9.2	−47.0	−107.0	−118.0

Sources: The Economic Report of the President, 1985; US Department of Commerce, 'The International Investment Position of the United States in 1985', Survey of Current Business, June 1986, cited in *South*, December 1986.

This committee had been formed during the 1930s crisis, when, through lack of co-ordination, the 12 regional Federal Reserve Banks had been unable to deal with the financial chaos. Set up as private banks with the power to control the money supply in each region, these regional Feds had had complete autonomy. But, while Roosevelt's New Deal kept them as private banks, it also set up a committee made up of 12 governors, including five heads of regional Feds, one of whom had to be the head of the New York Fed. This committee had the authority to impose unified monetary policies.

In highly confidential meetings, called eight times a year, the Open Market Committee used to alter by some tenths of a percentage point the interest rate on funds passed back to the banks (the discount rate) or the proportion of bank deposits that had to be left with the Fed as a compulsory reserve. This fine-tuning, carried out in anticipation of recessionary or inflationary upsurges, depended to a large extent on the bankers' intuition and to a lesser extent on Keynesian theories, developed during the Depression, according to which employment rose, within acceptable limits, in proportion to inflation.

But the crisis seemed to have overturned all these theories. Both inflation and unemployment rose at the same time and to unacceptable levels. Big corporations no longer respected the Fed's monetary policies, getting round limits by raising resources on the euromarket through their subsidiaries. And the authorities, accustomed to the post-war boom, were highly reluctant to carry out unpopular anti-inflationary policies, preferring to accumulate debts. The small public deficit of yesteryear became enormous.

The Brazilian economists Maria da Conceição Tavares and Luiz Gonzaga Belluzzo believe that Keynesianism — and indeed the whole of post-war economic thought — has proved incapable of dealing with the chaotic fluctuations in interest and exchange rates caused by the collapse of the gold standard and the floating interest rates on the euromarket.[17] Neither the demand for credit nor the level of economic activity seemed to respond any more to fine adjustments in interest rates. As the economist Stanley Black has said:

> For generations the Fed had used short-term interest rates as an intermediary variable that indicated the direction in which it wanted monetary policy to evolve . . . but gradually it began to realise that in periods of inflation nominal interest rates differed greatly from real interest rates, and it is these which are much more important for investors . . .[18]

The new monetarism

The apparent inability of Keynesianism to deal with the new situation brought back into fashion the old conservative monetarist theories that, as we have seen, had done so much harm to Latin America in the 1960s and 1970s. Refashioned by Milton Friedman, the new monetarism claimed that interest rates did not affect the level of economic activity in the US and that only rigid control over the money supply — that is, over the quantity of money and other means of payment in circulation — would bring down inflation. 'Both monetarists, who had been demanding this for a long time, and non-monetarists felt at the end of 1979 that it made sense to concentrate on the money supply', said Stanley Black.

For some time, Volcker had been asking Fed staff for studies on a possible change in philosophy and methods. Everything came together in the meeting on 6 October 1979, when a radical new policy was adopted, later to be considered 'a revolution in US monetary policy'. Volcker set up a rigid scheme for monitoring the monetary base, which would not be allowed to grow by more than 8 per cent a year. As well as this, he increased the basic interest rate — the discount rate — by one percentage point, from 11 to 12 per cent. He also reduced liquidity on the financial market, increasing the compulsory reserves and creating a new reserve, of 8 per cent, to be raised on unconventional forms of credit.

The result was a violent monetary squeeze that sent interest rates through the ceiling — including prime rate, charged on most of Latin America's debt. It was such a forceful squeeze that, more than a year later, when the recently-elected Reagan was battling for Congress to approve his economic programme, his aides were still fearful of its impact.

> Instead of pacing the monetary slow-down over a period of six years, the Fed decreed a 75 per cent reduction in just one year. By November 1981, the main measure for the monetary base, known as M1-B, which is made up of the money supply and all kinds of check accounts, had shrunk greatly. . . [It was] a ferocious squeeze that, with the delay in the approval of tax cuts, would make recession inevitable,

said Paul Craig, one of Reagan's chief advisers at the time.[19]

It seems that Paul Volcker and the other Fed governors were concerned only with American inflation. 'Our policy, in a long-term viewpoint, is based on a very simple premise, documented by centuries of experience, that the inflationary process is linked to the excessive growth of money and credit', he told the National Press Club.[20] But the truth is that the only way out of the US crisis envisaged by those in power was precisely the one that hurt other countries most deeply, affecting the indebted countries of Latin America like an earthquake.

It may seem surprising that within the US itself so little concern was shown for the enormous increase in interest rates. But it must be remembered that in the US many kinds of interest can be deducted from income tax. As this deduction can be worth up to half the nominal value of the interest, the part effectively paid during periods of high interest and high inflation can even be less than inflation itself.[21] Thus, while Latin America was sinking under the weight of prime, a member of the US ruling elite was writing: 'We do not know, for instance, how much importance to attribute to the sharp increase in interest rates . . . those who receive interest payments are charged tax, those who pay interest can deduct it from tax . . .'[22]

Maria da Conceição and Belluzzo are certain that the real objective of the Fed's monetary policies was not to bring down inflation, as they claimed, but to restore the hegemony of the dollar.[23] In 1981, the Bank for International Settlements (BIS) formally warned Reagan that his monetary policies 'were causing difficulties to other countries and could lead to a breakdown in international economic cooperation', but Paul Craig, the presidential aide, advised Reagan not to give in to any pressure.[24]

Inflation, in fact, only fell two years later. For this to happen, another radical change was required: the approval by Congress of Reagan's economic recovery programme, which fitted in perfectly with the Fed's monetary policies. Ronald Reagan was elected in November 1980 in the wake of a conservative revival created by the worsening crisis. A new group of economists, who believed in a strange economic doctrine that was the very antithesis of Keynesianism, came to power with him. To ameliorate the Depression of the 1930s, which took place against a background of important strikes and with memories of the Bolshevik revolution still fresh, Keynes had proposed that the state should create employment by redistributing income a little from the rich to the poor. In contrast, Reagan's advisers made exactly the opposite proposal: to reduce taxation for the rich to encourage investment. The best summary of this doctrine is one given by Reagan himself in a television interview:

> When I still worked in Hollywood, after my first film every year, if I made a second one, I would reach the tax category of those who paid 90 per cent in income tax. So I used not to make a second film. It was all right for me, but the cameramen, the production staff, the painters all remained without jobs.

Reagan took $23 billion away from the poorest families and increased the income of the richest by $35 billion. And, to end the most severe recession since the beginning of the crisis, he adopted an expansionary fiscal policy, increasing greatly the government's expenditure, mainly in armaments. The treasury deficit almost doubled in relation to revenue, and was covered by heavy borrowing that put yet more pressure on interest rates. It was the counter-revolution on the economic plane, led by the so-called 'supply-siders', who won this name for their policy of favouring those who controlled the means of production and of encouraging the supply of jobs rather than controlling demand for goods.

Just as in the domestic realm the supply doctrine transferred income from the poor to the rich, so in the international sphere it transferred income from the Third World to the First.

> The Reagan administration believes that income redistribution has been overly stressed, as much in industrialised countries as in the Third World, at the expense of policies for increasing income. The economic destiny of the Third World is to be freed of the international bureaucracy that supplies charity and to become the recipient of productive private investment,

said Paul Craig in a memo to Reagan.[25]

The international transfer of income

But how does this transfer of income, from the workers of the Third World to the rich of the First World, take place in practice? The increase in interest rates was part of an aggressive foreign policy, that tried to demonstrate to international capital that the only safe place in the world for their money was American territory. In this way, it sucked in capital from all over the world, including the billions of dollars that had left the United States when the country was building up its economic empire. Reagan launched a big armaments programme with the MX inter-continental missile, a new bomber and Star Wars. He reactivated the CIA as a centre of clandestine military operations and began openly to support the UNITA rebels in Angola, the *contras* in Nicaragua and the rebel forces in Afghanistan. Over half a billion dollars were spent training and equipping counter-revolutionaries in various parts of the world.[26]

The US bombed ports in Nicaragua, invaded the small island of Grenada, organised the overthrow of Baby Doc in Haiti and of Ferdinand Marcos in the Philippines, bombed Libya and sent troops to Bolivia to combat the drugs traffic. Reagan sabotaged disarmament talks with the Soviets for six years until 1987, infringed the nuclear test ban and denounced the Helsinki agreement over strategic arms controls. In the economic field, he exploited the debt crisis, rejecting every attempt at a long-term solution and opposing endeavours to expand the role of the Inter-American Development Bank (IDB) and the World Bank.[27] There was one main objective behind these varied initiatives: 'To remind investors of the dollar's virtues as a safe refuge', according to the US economist Fred Bergsten.[28]

Alarmed by the world instability (which the Reagan administration itself had largely created) and attracted by the high interest rates, capital from all over the world flowed to the United States, reaching $11.6 billion in 1982, $36.6 billion in 1983 and no less than $100.2 billion in 1984. So world savings were used to finance both the growing US trade deficit and the US public deficit, which was growing ever bigger, largely as the result of the increased military expenditure needed to finance the new interventionist role abroad. By attracting financial capital, instead of exporting it as in the past, the US helped to stop the flow of voluntary capital to Latin America.

But this was not the main consequence of the new policy. The race of investors to the US increased demand for dollars, firstly stopping the fall of the dollar on the exchange markets and then causing the dollar to rise. So another anomaly was created. Normally an economy with a balance of payments crisis devalues its currency to make its products cheaper abroad — this was the action taken by Nixon during the first phase of the US crisis. But with Reaganomics the opposite happened: the dollar rapidly appreciated. By the end of 1983, it had gone up 40 per cent, from its low-point in October 1979. This super-appreciation of the dollar, while the decadent US economy ran huge and growing trade deficits, broke all the laws of economics. Some economists believe that, as well as the unnaturally high interest rates in the US and the demonstration effect of Reagan's foreign policy, the Fed was manipulating the market to push the dollar up even higher.[29]

This super-dollar was an essential element in Reaganomics. But, while it successfully postponed the need for a definitive solution to the American crisis, it was the logic of the absurd. It increasingly allowed cheaper foreign goods to swamp the US market. It is not clear whether Reaganomics deliberately set out to close down less efficient US companies or whether this was simply the consequence of the need to attract dollars from all over the world to cover the deficit. The fact is that by 1984 a quarter of vehicles and steel consumed in the US and a third of machinery and textile products came from abroad.[30] It has been calculated that for each percentage point the dollar rose on the foreign markets, the US lost $3 billion in its trade surplus. The trade deficit reached $148 billion in 1984, $134 billion in 1985, $156 billion in 1986 and $171 billion in 1987.

Latin America had a key role in this mechanism, for the region's debt-servicing payments provided the US banks with a considerable part of the dollars required to cover the public deficit while its increased exports helped to supply the US market with cheap goods. In the first period of Reaganomics, 1981—84, Latin America's interest payments totalled $127.9 billion, equivalent to 15 per cent of the entire US military budget during this period or to 25 per cent of the accumulated US public deficit in the four years. Over 60 per cent of Latin America's interest bill was paid by its export surplus (*see* Table 1.1, p. 3).

The US became increasingly a nation of usurers. Financial income — that is, income from investment in financial transactions — rose from 26 per cent of national income in 1979 to 34 per cent in 1983. The percentage of personal income coming from interest doubled in five years.[31] It was as if the US was resigned to losing its role as world industrial leader and had decided to live from usury. US financial income grew spectacularly, and, together with other capital income, such as royalties and dividends, helped to offset part of the trade deficit. It has been calculated that, in the first half of the 1980s, for every one dollar of the trade deficit, the US received $1.1 in net income from capital income and services. It was, once again, the dance of the millions, with the creation both abroad and within the US of a new class of rentiers, that is, people living not from wages paid for their labour, but from interest or dividend.

All this postponed the crisis, but made sure that the crisis would be worse when it finally broke. 'The continual sequence of large deficits projected until after the end of this decade constitutes a serious threat to the economic recovery', warned Martin Feldstein, head of the president's economic advisory team, in 1983. By 1986, the US public debt had reached $1,700 billion, of which almost half was foreign ($860 billion). But by then, as we shall see in the next chapter, Feldstein's warnings were about to be vindicated.[32]

Notes

1. John Maynard Keynes, *Economic Consequences of the Peace*, Labour Research Department, 1920, p. 133.
2. Stephen Kanitz, 'Um Plano para a Dívida Externa Brasileira', mimeo, 1983.
3. Ernane Galvêas, *O Estado de S. Paulo*, 22 July 1984.
4. Albert Fishlow, *Adjustment Crisis in the Third World*, Transaction Books, 1984.
5. Philippe Collier, in *The Economist*, 13 June 1984.
6. William Cline, *International Debt*, MIT Press, 1984.
7. IMF's monthly letter, May 1986.
8. IMF press release, mimeo, 9 November 1982.
9. William C. Melton, *Inside the Fed*, Dow-Jones Irwin, 1985, p.184.
10. For interest rates in Great Britain during the last century, see R. Hilferding, *El Capital Financiero*, Madrid, Tecnos, 1973; for interest rates in the USA from 1930, see *The Economic Report of the President*, 1975. According to these sources, nominal interest rates of over 5 per cent occurred in Great Britain only in 1864 and 1866 and

in the USA in the 1930s and from 1967 onwards.

11. Jay W. Forrester, *The Futurist*, June 1985.

12. Sosa-Rodrigues, *Problèmes Structurelles des Relations Economiques Internationales de l'Amérique Latine*, Genève, Droz, 1963. According to this source, real interest rates reached as high as 10 per cent during this period.

13. Michael Moffitt, *O Dinheiro do Mundo*, Paz e Terra.

14. David P. Calleo, *The Imperious Economy*, Harvard University Press, 1982.

15. According to Per Drucker, in *Gazeta Mercantil*, 21 October 1985, about one third of the US trade loss was due to the fall in agricultural prices.

16. David P. Calleo, op. cit.

17. The magazine *Senhor*, 27 February 1985.

18. Stanley Black, in *The Global Repercussion of US Monetary and Fiscal Policy*, Ballinger Publishing Co., 1984.

19. Paul Craig, *The Supply Side Revolution*, Harvard University Press, 1984.

20. In Washington, 2 January 1980.

21. For example, with an interest rate of 20 per cent and inflation of 12 per cent, the 50 per cent of interest effectively paid (10 per cent) would be less than inflation.

22. US Congress Economic Report, 1980.

23. The magazine *Senhor*, 27 February 1985.

24. Paul Craig, op. cit.

25. Ibid.

26. Richard Newfarmer, in *From Gunboats to Diplomacy*, Johns Hopkins University Press, 1984.

27. Sidney Blumenthal, in the *Guardian Weekly*, 27 July 1985.

28. Fred Bergsten, *The US in the World Economy*, Lexington Books, 1983.

29. Kenneth King, in *US Monetary Policy and European Responses in the 80s*, Royal Institute of International Affairs, 1982, said that 'US intervention in the exchange markets lasted until the end of 1980'. David Calleo, op. cit., said that since 1961 the Fed had been intervening in the exchange market.

30. Mike Davis, *New Left Review*, No. 149, Jan–Feb 1984.

31. Ibid.

32. Martin Feldstein, in *The Global Repercussions of US Monetary Policy*, Ballinger Publishing Company, 1984.

10. The Renegotiation Crisis

How, one by one, the Latin American countries capitulated, victims of the rescheduling blackmail

> . . . When the international bankers indicate that they are prepared to make loans to a developing country, they are indicating their intention to go on gradually extending their loans forever . . . The worst of all possible attitudes that the international financial community can take towards a developing country is to alternate periods of excessive loans with periods without the concession of any new loans.
>
> **Jacques de Larosière**, former managing director of the IMF

Just as it was excessive world liquidity that allowed Latin America to accumulate its debt mountain, so it was the sudden cessation of this liquidity that finally brought the crisis to a head in 1982. Even before the Falklands/Malvinas war in April 1982, which many bankers later claimed was the reason why they reduced their loans, there were clear signs that, with the increase in interest rates, the era of abundant loans for Latin America was coming to an end. In the USA, important banks like Drysdale Securities and Penn Central, and big corporations like Chrysler and International Harvester, faced difficulties. In Argentina, several banks went bankrupt. Financial groups ran into problems in Chile. The Alfa group in Mexico had to be bailed out. Bolivia and Costa Rica did not manage to meet all the service payments due on their debt.

By early 1982, it was clear to many government officials in Latin America and bankers in the industrialised countries that the game was up. Though very few were prepared to admit it publicly, many bankers became increasingly concerned about their own vulnerability, fearful that a generalised default by Latin American nations could spark off a crash in the world's banking system. Their fears were exacerbated by the precarious nature of much of their lending to Latin America. It has been estimated that only 34 per cent of US commercial loans to Latin America had gone to governments. The rest was divided between local banks (29 per cent) and private sector companies (37 per cent).[1] Though the situation varied from country to country, much of the lending to non-government bodies had only the flimsiest of government guarantees or none at all. It became evident that, if recession were to hit Latin America and many local banks and companies become insolvent, foreign banks would be seriously hurt.

The situation deteriorated steadily in the first half of 1982. Bank lending to Latin America fell dramatically, as banks tried belatedly to reduce their vulnerability. Fearful of sparking off a world financial crisis, Latin American governments increasingly resorted to the only form of new finance available to them — short-term debt, with a repayment period of less than one year. This debt, which was supposed to be used by banks to cover temporary cash-flow shortages, could be raised easily on the inter-bank market without protracted negotiations. It was not intended to cover balance of payments deficits, but increasingly it was diverted to this use. But the relief was short-lived: the debt had to be repaid very soon, so the government had to increase yet more its borrowings on the inter-bank market. Latin American debt began to snowball even more quickly than in the past. At one stage, Brazil even encouraged the New York agencies of the big private Brazilian banks to take overnight deposits, that is, surplus cash deposited for a day or a week. This borrowing by Brazil alone, which did not form part of the country's registered foreign debt, reached $10 billion at one stage.[2] It has been estimated that by the middle of 1982 one-third of the total Latin American debt was made up of short-term loans.

Mexico was particularly vulnerable, because it had also been badly hurt by the slump in oil prices. Though the Mexican declaration of insolvency in August 1982 seemed to take some bankers by surprise, the crisis had a long incubation. Finance Minister Silva Herzog traced it back to July 1981, when the first drop in oil prices took place: 'It was then that the first dark clouds appeared on the horizon', he said.[3]

From early 1982, Mexican government officials, aware of the seriousness of the approaching crisis, had turned to the US government for help. But, because of their remarkable belief in the power of the market, US treasury officials had been slow to grasp the real dimensions of the crisis. 'The market will take care of you', Beryl Sprinkel, at that time under-secretary for monetary affairs, had said reassuringly to Mexican officials. Much later a White House official explained, somewhat ruefully: 'The reason Silva Herzog had to create an international crisis was to get the attention of the Treasury. The only way he could make them understand that something was up was by hitting them on the head.' A study of the crisis, published by the Group of 30, a group of leading developing countries, commented: 'The dialogue of the deaf averted any chance of a Mexican rescue short of a full-blown crisis.'

Though ignorance and ideological narrow-mindedness undoubtedly played a part, it seems that some US government officials at least were quite content to see Mexico reach the point of insolvency before agreeing to a rescue plan, for they believed that this would increase US bargaining power. A memo, dated 26 June 1982, which is believed to have been cleared with Thomas Enders, then Assistant Secretary of State for Inter-American Affairs, stated, with respect to Mexican criticisms of US Central American policy:

> With the wind out of its sails, Mexico is likely to be less adventuresome in its foreign policy and less critical of ours . . . It may be willing to sell more oil and gas at better prices, it may ease its restrictions on foreign investment, it may be prepared to negotiate a reciprocal reduction in tariffs and other trade barriers and it may even be willing to co-operate in managing illegal migration problems.[4]

The US intention of squeezing political and economic advantage out of Mexico's difficulties could scarcely be stated more clearly.

The Mexican crash

When the crisis finally broke in August 1982, a rescue package was put together with reasonable efficiency. Despite the haste, it established the pattern for future reschedulings, with functions distributed between the creditor governments, the banks and the IMF. The bankers had burnt their fingers badly in an earlier attempt to organise alone, without the IMF, a rescheduling package for a developing country. In March 1976, the US banks had agreed to reschedule Peru's debt and to provide new money, provided that the Peruvian government carried out an adjustment programme that they, the banks, had drawn up and were prepared to monitor. The experiment ended in disaster. The banks were accused of 'Wall Street imperialism', while the Peruvian economy went from bad to worse. The banks, led by Morgan Guaranty, decided that from then on they would retire to the wings, leaving the IMF centre stage to face the barrage of criticism.[5]

So, this time round, there was a clear allocation of tasks. The creditor governments, together with the Bank for International Settlements (BIS), became responsible for averting an immediate banking crisis by providing short-term bridging finance. The IMF worked out how much debt needed to be restructured, how tough an austerity programme could be imposed on the Mexican economy and how much new money was required from the commercial banks to avoid another insolvency crisis. The banks worked out the terms of the rescheduling — the spreads, the commission and the other fees. All three sectors firmly declared that the condition for Mexico's rescue was that it negotiated an austerity programme with the IMF.

The situation was alarming, for, with the very heavy loans that many of the world's leading banks had made to Mexico (*see* Tables 10.1 and 10.2), it was evident that a Mexican default could spark off a world banking crisis, particularly if its action was copied by other Latin American debtors. But both the banks and the US government did surprisingly little to protect world financial stability, but acted instead to look after their own immediate interests. The banks took advantage of the panic to create a steering committee to co-ordinate their actions. It was a move that greatly strengthened their position and was to be copied later in respect of the other debtor nations. As one observer has pointed out: 'The connivance inherent in this committee gave each bank a monopoly power that did not exist at the time when the borrower originally contracted its debt'.[6]

Instead of granting soft credit terms, as often happens when a domestic customer in the industrialised countries faces repayment difficulties, the steering committees insisted on charging considerably more than normal for their loans and services, claiming that the 'risks' had increased. Mexico (and, later, all other Latin American debtors) was fearful of doing anything that could antagonise the US government or the banks, so it did not even hire an independent firm of financial consultants to represent it in the negotiations with the banks, as insolvent US companies routinely did. All in all, Mexico finished up paying an enormous 13 per cent interest on its refinanced debt, a rate that was regarded as scandalous even at the time.

The US government was just as opportunistic as the banks. Its $1 billion payment to the Mexican government for advance oil purchases was made under exorbitant conditions, equivalent to an annual interest rate of 30 per cent. Even President Reagan is said to have complained to Donald Regan, the US Secretary of the Treasury, about the harshness of the terms. To which Regan reportedly replied:

'No, Mr President. I'm not hard-hearted. I just want to give the American tax-payer the same kind of service I gave the stockholders of Merrill Lynch' (the financial firm in Wall Street that Regan earlier headed).

Perhaps surprisingly, in view of the reputation for harshness it was later to win in Latin America, the IMF behaved with considerable caution and moderation during this first rescheduling. Unlike the US government and the banks, it appears to have been deeply concerned that Mexico, if pushed beyond reasonable limits, could decide on unilateral measures. It was rumoured at the time — and later confirmed by Mexican cabinet minutes, quoted in a *Panorama* programme on British television — that the Mexican government had held two meetings with Brazilian and Argentine government officials. Mexico apparently proposed that Latin America's three largest debtors should simultaneously declare a moratorium on debt payments so as to increase their bargaining power. Much to the IMF's relief, the idea was turned down by both Brazil and Argentina. But the IMF nevertheless took a lenient line. 'Mexico breathes a sigh of relief' was the headline in the *Financial Times*[7] when the terms of the adjustment programme were finally announced. But all in all the salvage operation, which was to be copied time and again in the long series of Latin American reschedulings carried out over the following 18 months, was decidedly tough.

Brazil follows suit

The banks and the IMF went to considerable lengths to prevent several big Latin American debtors ceasing payments simultaneously, as this clearly could have pushed the world banking system to breaking point. They paid lip service to the blatantly hollow declaration by Brazil's finance minister, Ernane Galvêas, in September 1982: 'Brazil is different from Argentina, different from Mexico, different from all the others'.[8] In what can only have been a deliberate move to avoid bunching, the banks provided Brazil with $2.8 billion in fresh money in the third quarter of 1982, while Mexico, which was rescheduling its debt and submitting to an IMF programme, received only $1.8 billion.

But by the end of November 1982, with the Mexican problem temporarily under control, the banks turned their attention to Brazil. Despite the bail-outs from the banks, Brazil had been all but insolvent for two months. There had been one period in September — nicknamed the 'Black Week' — when the New York subsidiary of the Bank of Brazil actually ran out of funds and had to be bailed out by the Federal Reserve Board. The military government, headed by General João Figueiredo, maintained the farce that Brazil was 'different', partly because it lacked the political courage to face up to its creditors before all other options were totally exhausted and partly because it was anxious not to call in the IMF before the congressional elections in mid-November. Such a move would have completely wrecked the already slim chances of the pro-military party, the PDS.

By this time, both the IMF and the banks were more confident in what they somewhat smugly named 'crisis management' and were prepared to treat Brazil even more harshly than Mexico. The terms and conditions of the agreement to reschedule $4.7 billion and to lend a further $4.4 billion, imposed on Brazil by the banks' steering committee, co-ordinated by Anthony Gebauer, a director of Morgan Guaranty Trust, can only be called extortionate. A spread of 2.125 per cent above Libor was charged on public debts and of 2.5 per cent on private debts. This difference alone, compared with the 1.75 per cent negotiated with Mexico just a few weeks earlier, cost Brazil another $68 million for loans that were no more expensive for the banks to make. For loans charged at the US prime rate, the spread was 1.875 per cent. The banks could choose between prime and Libor.

An exorbitant commission of 1.5 per cent, triple the normal rate, was also charged. This commission is discounted from disbursement, so that, out of a loan of 100, the debtor receives only 98.5, though he has to repay 100 and pay interest on 100. This 1.5 per cent commission meant an additional interest payment of 0.1 per cent, or $9.1 million a year. The way of working out the floating interest rate on the Brazilian money was stated in the Deposit Facility Agreement, signed on 2 February 1983 between the Central Bank of Brazil and the creditor banks' steering committee, with Citibank acting as its agent. It became the standard method used in loan contracts with Latin American nations and is worth quoting. This method, it said, was to be used in the US to calculate the rate of interest:

Article 1
Section 1.01
. . . Dollar domestic rate means . . . a fluctuating interest rate per annum equal at all times to . . . the rate of interest announced publicly by Citibank in New York from time to time as the Citibank base rate . . .

A similar procedure was to be used in Britain:

Libor rate means . . . the average (rounded up if necessary to the nearest whole multiple of 1/16 of 1 per cent per annum) of the rates per annum at which deposits . . . are offered by each of the Libor reference banks to prime banks in the London inter-bank market at 11.00 a.m. (London time) two business days before . . . Libor reference banks mean the respective principal London offices of Citibank, the Industrial Bank of Japan Limited, Lloyds Bank International, Société Général and Union Bank of Switzerland.

In other words, it was the banks themselves that had a large say in determining the interest rate that was charged on Latin American debt. According to Stephen Kanitz, from the University of São Paulo, an increase in the rates offered on the inter-bank market in London can be noted just before 11 o'clock in the morning.[9] The additional gain to be made by the banks by rounding upwards the percentage could be equivalent to $180,000 a year, just on the $9.1 billion involved in the Brazilian rescheduling.

As if this was not enough, the committee demanded a free hand, in special circumstances, to set whatever interest rate it wanted:

Section 2.06
If the agent receives notice from at least 25 per cent of the banks that the Libor rate . . . will not adequately reflect the cost to such banks of maintaining or funding . . . the agent and the central bank should enter negotiations in good faith with a view to agreeing an alternative basis . . .

But it appears that the reference to 'good faith' was no more than a formality. For the following procedure was to be used to resolve any deadlock:

> If the agent and the central bank shall not have agreed on a substitute for Libor rate, the agent shall (after consultation with each such bank) give notice to the central bank of the new rate of interest.

In other words, the creditor banks could dictate whatever rate they wished. This clause was probably put in to please the small banks that might have higher costs than the big banks active on London's inter-bank market. But, despite this justification, Section 2.06 meant in practice that Brazil gave the banks a blank cheque. Moreover, it not only accepted the jurisdiction of New York courts to resolve any dispute, but also paid all the legal costs of the contract, including even a daily allowance for the lawyers, as well as shouldering all other expenses incurred during the negotiation. In this way, the Brazilian crisis became a source of additional profit for the banks — and perhaps also for the bankers. Anthony Gebauer, who was the representative of the banks in this first Brazilian rescheduling, confessed three years later to the Federal Tribunal of Justice in New York that he had been responsible for fraudulent deposits and withdrawals, involving Brazilian clients, worth \$4.3 billion.

One by one, the Latin American nations, starved of new funds, were forced to reschedule their debts and reach agreement with the IMF. Overwhelmed by the scale of their problems, none of the governments obtained real concessions from the creditors. But of all the governments, the Chilean was, paradoxically, both the one with the most leverage over the banks and the most subservient.

The Chilean capitulation

Because of the foreign bankers' blind trust in the Chicago Boys and their monetarist experiment, much foreign capital had entered the country in the 1970s outside the government's control. Though at the time this lending had been particularly profitable for the banks, it meant that in 1982 just over 80 per cent of the foreign debt was not guaranteed by the government, a much higher proportion than in other Latin American countries. With the local banks in such poor shape by this time, it seemed unlikely that the interest on most of this debt would be paid. Indeed, the debt was being sold at a discount of 30−40 per cent on the secondary market, that shadowy market where commercial banks discreetly sell, usually at a considerable discount, developing country debt that they no longer want to hold.

The high proportion of non-guaranteed debt should have given the Pinochet government a powerful card in its talks with its creditors. At the very least, the government could have obtained considerable concessions in spreads and commissions in return for a commitment to honour these debts. But the opportunity was thrown away. Under pressure from the banks, the government took over responsibility for these loans — in exchange for absolutely nothing. In its first rescheduling, it agreed to a spread of 2.16 per cent and a commission of 1.25

per cent, which were about the Latin American average. It was only in the third rescheduling in 1985 that it received a token reduction, of 0.5 per cent, in the fees it paid, in recognition of this guarantee.

Nor did the Pinochet government receive any compensation from the IMF for its model behaviour. Despite the fierce recession that the country had already been through in 1982, the IMF insisted on a conventional austerity programme, with further deflationary measures. Local economists believe that, far from winning him concessions, Pinochet's evident unwillingness to confront either the banks or the IMF only weakened his position, leading to an even tougher settlement.[10]

The end of the first round

By early 1984 and the end of what has become known as the first round of reschedulings, all Latin American nations but two — Colombia and Paraguay — had rescheduled their debts and called in the IMF. The austerity programmes negotiated with the IMF were remarkably tough, especially when compared with the rescue packages that were set up during the same period for large insolvent transnational companies, such as Chrysler. These packages were based on the assumption that, if the company was to overcome its crisis, it must be allowed to return to growth and profitability within a brief period. As a result, they routinely contained innovative features, such as interest rates set below the market level and the conversion of part of the debt into shares, all of which entailed some losses for the banks. But Latin American debtors were allowed none of these new features. As one observer has pointed out, 'the contrast is striking, especially when one recalls that the banks can put in a liquidator and wind up and sell off an enterprise while no truly analagous procedure is practical today with respect to sovereign borrowers'.[11]

But if the process was painful for Latin America, it was exceedingly profitable for the banks. During this first round of rescheduling, Latin America rescheduled loans worth an enormous $49.5 billion, more than the total value of all previous Latin American reschedulings. For the banks the new deals meant perhaps greater risks, but also extraordinary rates of profit, impossible in normal conditions. According to ECLAC, spreads averaged 2.25 per cent over Libor, with commissions of 1.25 per cent. This meant that, far from helping Latin America through a difficult period, the banks had doubled the cost of new loans, compared with 1980−81. As a result, they earned about $1.7 billion from these first reschedulings, which was a very high rate of profit, even by the standards of the banks, accustomed to a very good return on their Latin American lending (*see* box, p. 127).

The spectacle of the banks profiting at the expense of the Latin American people was distasteful to many observers, of many varied political views. The *Financial Times* commented in 1983, with the reschedulings in full swing: 'So we get reschedulings, with the accompaniment of vast telexes, higher interest rates, spreads and other fees, which make the whole problem in the long run just a little more unmanageable. The banks of course know this very well.'[12]

During this period, observers often asked why Latin America, with its mountain of debt, was proving so inept at wresting concessions from either the IMF or the banks. Anatole Kaletsky, a feature writer at the *Financial Times*, who followed the reschedulings closely, pointed to what undoubtedly was — and still is — the key factor: 'Debtors have not succeeded in pushing bankers anywhere near the theoretical limits of their involuntary lending capacity for one major reason: they have failed to convince the banks that default is a plausible option and hence a threat.'[13] Only on one occasion did the banks agree to favourable conditions for a Latin American borrower, with interest limited to 7 per cent and a five-year grace period on principal repayments. This was given to the revolutionary Sandinista government in Nicaragua: the banks knew that the Sandinistas had hesitated before accepting responsibility for the foreign debts of the Somoza dictatorship, which they had just overthrown, and, if harsh conditions were imposed, they could simply decide to repudiate the debt. In this case, and only in this case, default was plausible. Faced with a real challenge, the banks backed down.

The profitability of the lending did not, however, encourage the banks to resume lending to Latin America on a large scale. Total lending from all sources fell from $77.8 billion in 1981 to $40.3 billion in 1983 (*see* Table 2.2, p. 17). The banks, it became clear, would lend only under duress from the IMF and the creditor governments, and when they were convinced that the new loans would be immediately returned to them as interest payments. It was largely because of this drastic reduction in bank lending that Latin America became a net exporter of capital, at enormous social cost, as we have seen.

Such exorbitant profits, so blatantly extracted from the misery of the Latin American people, could not last indefinitely. Gradually and timidly, Latin American nations began to organise concerted action to demand some improvement in conditions. The first important meeting was held in Ecuador in January 1984. In the Declaration of Quito, the debtors did little more than ask for conditions similar to those now routinely provided for troubled transnationals. In particular, they asked for a ceiling on interest payments, longer maturities, more fresh money and easier access to the markets of the industrialised countries. In June, eleven debtor nations — Argentina, Bolivia, Brazil, Chile, Colombia, the Dominican Republic, Ecuador, Mexico, Peru, Uruguay and Venezuela — met in Colombia and set up what was to become known as the Cartagena group. Despite the alarm that the meeting caused among bankers in the industrialised countries, it was most notable for what it did not do: it did not form a debtors' cartel to make collective demands on the creditors; and it provided no more than formal support for Argentina, which was trying to stand up to its creditors. Indeed, the Argentine experience was soon to demonstrate clearly the difficulties that a country faced when trying to stand up to its creditors on its own.

Argentina has a go

Argentina first rescheduled its debt under military rule. In 1982, the military signed a letter of intent to the IMF in which they promised to undertake an adjustment programme in return for a $2-billion loan package, to be disbursed over 15 months.

The 325 creditor banks came in with a $1-billion bridging loan, and the BIS with $500 million. The adjustment programme was not particularly austere, by IMF standards, but the military government proved incapable of fulfilling the targets. The IMF delayed disbursement of some tranches of its loan, but in general seemed tolerant of the country's difficulties.

In January 1984, the civilian politician Raúl Alfonsín came to power, putting an end to eight years of military rule. The worst of the crisis seemed over. The foreign spending spree, which had led to the unprecedented trade deficit of $2.5 billion in 1980, had been brought under control. Imports had dropped from just over $10 billion in 1981 to under $5 billion in 1982. The country had returned to its traditional practice of running a healthy trade surplus ($2.7 billion in 1982). The government was confident that the country's economic recovery, together with the warm reception abroad that had been given to the new democratic regime, would mean that it would no longer be subjected to conventional austerity programmes. Raúl Prebisch, the veteran founder of ECLAC, who was advising Alfonsín, said in November 1983: 'Our return to democracy will help us obtain better conditions in the rescheduling.'

But Prebisch could not have been more mistaken. It soon became clear that the IMF had treated the military with velvet gloves because they could not be trusted to behave responsibly, but that this was not the case with Alfonsín. Jorge Schwarzer, an Argentine economist, put it as follows:

> A military government that had not thought twice about rushing into a war with Great Britain and that possessed a highly centralised and mysterious decision-making mechanism, might well decide to suspend foreign debt payments. Everything suggests that this was why it was treated with leniency. But, ironically, the Alfonsín government was much more predictable — an attribute which is generally seen as one of the advantages of democracy, but in this case simply meant that the creditors did not need to treat it with such care.[14]

When, in March 1983, Margaret Thatcher was asked by Michael Foot, then leader of the opposition, why Britain, still technically at war with Argentina, had contributed to the IMF package of new finance, she replied: 'In the absence of either the IMF or commercial loans, there was a possibility that Argentina would default. If she was to default, she would have even more money to spend on arms than if she met the debt. That is a fact of life.'[15] So it was fear of default that lay behind Britain's conciliatory attitude, and probably that of most other creditor nations.

Alfonsín had hoped to reach a rescheduling agreement with the banks without turning to the IMF. But his proposal provoked fierce opposition abroad. 'The international financial system operated in practice like a powerful cartel, demanding an agreement with the Fund as the basis for any renegotiation', commented Schwarzer.[16] By the end of March 1984, tension reached breaking point. The banks greatly increased their pressure, for they needed the government to start paying interest on their loans to prevent them from being classified as 'non-performing' in the banks' accounts. At the same time, the IMF insisted on a far tougher austerity programme than the one it had negotiated with the military. Bernardo Grinspun, the finance minister, protested: 'The Argentine government cannot be held responsible for the banks' accounting problems. The creditors cannot demand more from the democratic government than they did from the military.' But it was. And they did.

Apart from capitulation, the only viable option was to mobilise the country and prepare for outright confrontation with the creditors. But this tactic does not seem to have been seriously considered by the moderate, right-of-centre Alfonsín government. It had expected sympathy from its creditors and, when this was not forthcoming, it seemed incapable of toughening its stance at other than a rhetorical level.

The crisis was defused by a remarkable bridging loan, to which Mexico and Venezuela each contributed $100 million and Brazil and Colombia $50 million. It was presented as an act of Latin American solidarity, but, in practice, it bailed out the banks by averting any remaining chance of confrontation. Donald Regan, the US Secretary of the Treasury, was reported as saying, in relief: 'Argentina could have become an example to other countries, not only in Latin America, but in the rest of the world. But, thank goodness, that risk is over.'[17] The bridging loan had a sting in its tail. If in the future Argentina failed to reach agreement with the IMF and was thus unable to obtain fresh funds with which to repay the Latin American nations, it would be unable to present its conflict with the IMF as an anti-imperialist crusade. Rather, as a conservative Argentine paper put it, it would 'humiliate the country'.

The Argentine government tried for a few more months to defy — or at least to out-manoeuvre — the IMF, but, finally, in mid-1984, it capitulated. At the IMF's annual meeting in September, Grinspun said that he had reached agreement with the IMF. A few days later the interior minister told a meeting of businessmen in Buenos Aires that the country was doomed to '25 years of limitations', during which half of its export earnings, equivalent to about 7 per cent of the country's economic output, would have to be allocated to the servicing of the foreign debt.[18] It was the final admission of defeat from a government that had come to office with such high hopes just nine months earlier.

Multi-year reschedulings

Though Alfonsín's strategy ended in disaster, the banks' experience helped convince them of the dangers of repeated annual reschedulings. Sooner or later, they feared, one of the debtor governments would become exasperated — and exhausted — by the yearly wranglings and opt for all-out confrontation. Far better, they decided, to negotiate an agreement that would last several years, even if it did not bring them such a high rate of profit. It was in this way that 'multi-year reschedulings' were created and the pioneer, once again, was Mexico, which has consistently emerged as a trend-setter in the debt crisis, largely, it would seem, because of its 3,000-kilometre frontier with the US, which gives it exceptional leverage over its powerful neighbour to the north.

The deal broke new ground by rescheduling a large amount of money ($48.7 billion) over a long period (14 years), with no commission and a low spread (1.13 per cent). Though the deal eliminated the worst excesses of the first round of reschedulings, it still imposed a heavy burden. Nothing was done to alleviate the interest payments, which were still running at $10−11 billion, equivalent to 6 per cent of the country's economic output. Worse still, repayments of capital were due to increase to about $5−6 billion in 1990. Experienced observers cautioned that Mexico would simply be unable to honour such commitments for more than a year or two. These warnings were vindicated much sooner than expected. In the autumn of 1985 the collapse in world oil prices made it impossible for Mexico to keep to the terms of the deal. By then, a new development — the Peruvian initiative — had added a new and explosive element to the debt crisis.

By early 1985, as a result of falling living standards, social discontent was growing in Peru, as in many other Latin American nations. Trade unions and neighbourhood groups, often linked to the progressive wing of the Catholic Church, began to express this unrest politically.[19] Taking advantage of the new mood, Alan García, leader of the APRA party, ran in the presidential elections in April 1985 on a nationalist, if imprecise, programme of social reform and confrontation with the foreign creditors. After winning a decisive victory, García unexpectedly announced in July a tough new debt policy in which he promised not to negotiate any more austerity programmes with the IMF and to limit payments in debt-servicing to 10 per cent of foreign exchange earnings.

His programme was not revolutionary, nor even strongly reformist. His main objective, it appears, was to relieve the country of the enormous debt burden so that he would have the resources to modernise the economy and carry out social welfare programmes. But the banks were angry and alarmed. At $13.8 billion, Peru's foreign debt was not large enough to inflict crippling losses on the banks' annual accounts. But, if Peru succeeded in reducing its debt burden by such radical action, other more powerful debtors, such as Brazil or Mexico, could follow suit. It was the possible 'export' of the Peruvian model that alarmed them.

There were other signs of revolt in Latin America. In August 1985, Fidel Castro held an impassioned conference in Havana in which speaker after speaker denounced the suffering caused by the debt crisis and called on Latin American governments to repudiate their debts, or, at the very least, to declare a temporary moratorium so as to regain the political initiative. Most of the participants in the conference were opposition leaders, with very little real power. But the enthusiasm with which their message was received by some sectors of the Latin American population clearly worried the bankers.

The Baker Plan

The time had clearly come for a new move by the industrialised countries to prevent the Latin American rebellion, still very weak, from gaining momentum. It was against this background that James Baker, the US Treasury Secretary, launched at the annual IMF−World Bank meeting in October 1985 an initiative to alleviate the debt problem in 15 troubled middle-income debtor nations, of which ten were Latin American (Argentina, Bolivia, Brazil, Chile, Colombia, Ecuador, Mexico, Peru, Uruguay and Venezuela). He said that if these countries adopted market-oriented adjustment policies (which had become the code term for IMF programmes), $29 billion in additional funding would be provided, partly from the commercial banks ($20 billion) and partly from the official financial institutions ($9 billion).

This initiative, which became known as the Baker Plan, was essentially an attempt to counteract the alarming decline in lending by the banks, which had become even more marked in 1984 and 1985, falling to just one-third of its level in the 1979−81 period (*see* Table 2.2, p. 17). It had become evident that some big debtors, starved of new funds, might soon have had little option but to declare a moratorium. By encouraging additional lending, Baker hoped to lessen the possibility of radical action by a major debtor. Though it was presented exclusively as an initiative to help the debtor nations, the plan seems to have been drawn up with the interests of the banks foremost in Baker's mind.

But the Baker plan proved too timid an initiative to change the pattern of events, which in 1986 and 1987 began to take quite another course. In September 1985, Mexico experienced its worst ever earthquake, which killed 20,000 people and required an outlay of $3 billion in reconstruction costs. At the same time, the drastic fall in world oil prices cut by half Mexico's oil earnings, still its main source of foreign currency. Despite everything, President Miguel de la Madrid tried to carry on with debt-servicing payments. Anatole Kaletsky commented in the *Financial Times*:

> If it was not so tragic, it would be almost comic. In response to the most serious natural disaster this century, Mexico is increasing taxes, cutting public expenditure and squeezing wherever possible its economy. No price seems high enough, no sacrifice sufficient, to maintain the confidence of international creditors.[20]

But it was an unequal struggle. In February 1986, de la Madrid said that a third debt deal would be sought, with much softer payment conditions. Baker tried to present the new initiative as the first concrete result of his plan, but in practice it dealt a death blow to the lingering hopes that the plan might work. For under the new deal, which took 13 months of bitter wrangling to complete, Mexico managed to convince the banks to accept a linkage between Mexico's internal growth rate, oil prices and the amount that Mexico could pay in debt service. In other words, the banks agreed for the first time to accept that external conditions on the world market could present a debtor country with legitimate reasons for making less than full debt payments. In practice, this had been the case with many debtor nations since the outbreak of the crisis in mid-1982, but many of the creditors, particularly the US regional banks and the four British high-street banks, were very unhappy with the explicit linkage and were very unlikely to resume voluntary lending in such circumstances. Indeed, the deal was only completed in February 1987, after the unexpected declaration of a moratorium by the Brazilian government had resurrected the old spectre of a debtors' cartel. Reverting to their old 'divide and rule' tactics, the banks were anxious to resolve, at least temporarily, the Mexican question so that they could concentrate their minds on Brazil.

But even before the Brazilian scare, the banks had had second thoughts about the Baker Plan, if they had ever paid more than lip-service to it. As it became evident that the debtor nations would demand more and more concessions, the banks, particularly those in a strong financial position, began to resist strongly any move to divert them away from what, in practice, had been their policy since mid-1982: a slow retreat from Latin America. It became clear that, during the first few years of the debt crisis, the commercial banks had gone along with the reschedulings, even those entailing the outlay of additional new money, because they needed time to build up their strength. Left alone, the banks would probably have paced their retreat even more cautiously, but the Brazilian moratorium acted as a catalyst.

Brazil suspends debt payments

The Brazilian moratorium on interest payments, declared in February 1987, was the most radical move hitherto made by a Latin American debtor. Yet, ironically, this momentous step was taken by a timid and conservative president, who failed to mobilise public opinion around the initiative, which he had taken only after all other alternatives seemed exhausted. With hindsight, it seems difficult to imagine a less propitious setting for confrontation with the bankers and the creditor governments.

In 1985, after refusing to negotiate an austerity agreement with the IMF, Brazil pulled off a remarkable coup, combining one of the highest rates of growth in the western world (8.2 per cent) with a large trade surplus ($12.5 billion), which enabled it to pay the interest on its foreign debt. But the strain of performing well on both the domestic and external fronts soon became visible. Domestic investment fell to a dangerously low level, while inflation spiralled out of control. Under the leadership of finance minister Dilson Funaro, the government drew up the Cruzado Plan, a daring attempt to combat the internal causes of this inflation, while maintaining rapid economic growth. Such an approach was anathema to the IMF, and, knowing this, the Brazilian government did not even submit the plan.

In its early draft, the plan also included a much tougher stance on the external front. The team of young economists who were advising Funaro argued that it was essential to attack on both the external and internal fronts simultaneously, to prevent the strain of debt-servicing creating inflationary pressures of the kind described in Chapter 2. They also argued that the very size of Brazil's debt, the largest in the developing world, gave it considerable bargaining power, sufficient to wrest meaningful concessions from the country's creditors, without the need to turn to the IMF.

The economist Paulo Nogueira Batista, one of Funaro's top aides, calculated that Brazil had made a net transfer abroad of $34 billion in the three-year period 1983−85 (a calculation comparable to our calculations of $30 billion, *see* Table 8.2, p. 79). The transfer, he argued, was equivalent to sending abroad each year 5 per cent of the country's economic output. In this economist's view, it was the main reason why domestic investment, which had run at an average rate of 22 per cent of gross domestic product in the 1960s and 1970s, had dropped to the dangerously low rate of 16 per cent, far too low to permit annual growth of 7 per cent, which is generally acknowledged to be the minimum required to start tackling Brazil's serious social problems. With the support of Funaro, Paulo Nogueira Batista suggested that net capital remittance should be limited to 2.5 per cent of economic output, that is, to $5−6 billion a year.

But President Sarney did not have the political courage — or the leadership — required by the initial draft. Intimidated by the pressure from the creditors, President Sarney insisted that, in the final version, announced in February 1986, only the domestic measures should be included, apparently unaware that, by doing so, he was guaranteeing the plan's stillbirth. Instead of unilaterally setting a limit on debt remittances, he insisted that Brazil should try to reach a friendly agreement with the creditor banks over a more favourable rescheduling. But this was clearly impossible, given Brazil's refusal to negotiate an IMF programme and the banks' determination to teach Brazil a lesson. The banks became confident that all they needed was a little patience: the inherent contradiction between vigorous domestic growth and full payment of debt-servicing would eventually cause the Cruzado Plan to 'implode'.

And that was precisely what happened. Brazil was unable to maintain its heavy trade surplus under the Cruzado Plan and began to run down its foreign reserves so as to carry on with its debt-servicing payments. Finally, in February 1987, when the country had all but run out of foreign reserves, President Sarney belatedly declared a moratorium on debt payments. But he was unable to mobilise political support from either the left or the right of the political spectrum. Left-wing groups believed that his action amounted to 'too little too late', while right-wing sectors saw the moratorium as an unmitigated disaster because it antagonised the country's creditors. Instead, they argued that Brazil should give up all pretence at independence, accept another IMF austerity programme and then go back to the banks for a further conventional rescheduling package.

The banks build up their provisions

Despite President Sarney's failure to win support for the measure at home, the moratorium greatly worried foreign bankers — and for good reason. It seemed that finally their worst fears had been realised: with the biggest Latin American debtor no longer paying interest, banking regulations would soon force the big money-centre banks to declare their loans to Brazil as 'non-performing', that is, they would have to be considered as losses in the banks' accounts. Since 1982, the commercial banks had been slowly strengthening their capital base and increasing their provisions for Third World losses, but loans to Latin America still accounted for a large proportion of the shareholders' equity, which was the only asset that really belonged to the banks and could thus be called upon in emergencies (*see* Table 10.1). The Brazilian moratorium revealed, embarrassingly, the continued vulnerability of the banks.

Brazil's action seems to have strengthened the resolve of the stronger and more profitable banks, particularly Citicorp, the largest private US banking group, to take drastic action to protect this dangerous chink in their armour. At the same time, Citicorp must have been aware of the possible strategic advantage of being first in the field. By taking dramatic and unexpected action to reduce its vulnerability, Citicorp would force its competitors to follow suit. As some, such as Bank of America, would be hard-pressed to find the resources to do so, Citicorp would emerge in an even stronger position.

Table 10.1
The weight of Latin American debt in the nine leading US money-centre banks
(value of outstanding loans in $ bn) (end 1984)

	Mexico	Brazil	Venezuela	Argentina	Chile	Five countries' total	Five countries' loan as % of shareholders' equity
Bank America	2.7	2.5	1.5	0.5	0.3	7.5	145.1
Citicorp	2.9	4.8	1.4	1.2	0.5	10.8	178.6
Chase Manhattan	1.6	2.7	1.2	0.8	0.5	6.8	198.3
Manufacturers Hanover	1.9	2.2	1.1	1.3	0.7	7.2	254.7
Morgan Guaranty	1.2	1.8	0.5	0.8	0.3	4.6	134.5
Continental Illinois	0.7	0.5	0.4	0.4	0.3	2.3	124.5
Chemical	1.4	1.3	0.8	0.4	0.4	4.3	179.6
Bankers' Trust	1.3	0.7	0.4	0.3	0.3	3.0	166.8
First Chicago	0.8	0.7	0.2	0.2	0.2	2.1	116.3
Total	**14.5**	**17.2**	**7.5**	**5.9**	**3.5**	**48.6**	**166.5**

Source: Anatole Kaletsky, *The Costs of Default*, Priority Press, New York, 1985.

So, at the end of April, Citicorp surprised the world banking community by announcing its decision to take a $2.5-billion loss in the second quarter of the year so as to increase its loan loss reserves from $2 billion to $5 billion. Citicorp's move was widely copied. This had a certain irony, given that Citicorp had been at the very front of the lending binge in the 1970s. As one commentator pointed out:

> They [the other commercial banks] have been forced into the invidious position of having to acknowledge their previous lack of prudence by none other than Citicorp — Citicorp, the Pied Piper who led the world's banks into lending to the developing world in the first place, assuring doubters through thick and a great deal of thin that 'countries cannot go bankrupt'.[21]

Five of the next six largest US banks each set aside at least $1 billion in additional reserves. The four big banks in Britain together set aside £3.4 billion. Lloyds and Midland, the most-heavily exposed of the British banks, had to make the heaviest provisions, of £1,066 million and £916 million respectively. As a result, the two banks showed losses, of £248 million and £505 million respectively, in their 1987 accounts. These were the first losses ever reported by clearing banks in modern times. For Lloyds, the move was particularly embarrassing; as recently as April

1987, Sir Jeremy Morse, its chief executive, had pooh-poohed concern over the Brazilian moratorium, stating in public that the financial condition of Brazil was 'more healthy than that of the Republic of Ireland'. As the same commentator pointed out, after Lloyds had announced its extraordinary increase in provisions, 'What, one wonders, will it now provide against its Irish exposure?'[22] Midland, in its turn, had to sell its Scottish and Irish assets to raise the funds, and, even so, left itself vulnerable to being taken over by another group, possibly a foreign bank.

But the impact of the Brazilian moratorium proved to be far wider. As a result of their emergency actions, the value of the shares of some of the big banking groups fell on the US stock market, raising some of the first doubts as to the destiny of the huge, inflated US stock market, which, fuelled by the precarious prosperity created by Reaganomics, had shown extraordinary growth. And the decline in the banks' shares by itself encouraged a further fall, for it reduced the value of the banks' assets with respect to their Latin American lending. The nervousness also affected the dollar, which fell further on the world's exchange markets.

The knock-on effect continued into the summer. Three months after the Brazilian moratorium, after the completion of the first 90 days, which is the maximum period permitted to banks to receive no interest on a loan before they have to classify it as 'non-performing', the Federal Reserve Board had to bail out the largest Texan bank, the First City Bank Corporation, which had net capital assets of only $480 million, against 'non-performing' loans of $1.1 billion. The nervousness increased, as investors began to fear that the Dow Jones index might not reach 3,000, that abstract threshhold that had taken on symbolic importance with no basis in the real world.

Finally, the crash happened. On 'Black Monday', the instantly legendary 19 October 1987, investors, particularly foreign investors, pulled out of dollar investments, and the New York exchange fell by a record 22.6 per cent in a single day, more than double the drop on the fateful 'Black Thursday' in 1929. The financial press began to talk of the possibility that the stock market 'meltdown' could spark off a world financial crisis, when, in fact, the crisis already existed in the periphery and was itself one of the causes of the stock market crash.

By then, paradoxically, the Brazilian moratorium had proved to be yet another false alarm. After Funaro resigned in July, Brazil's debt policy became more and more conventional, first under Luiz Carlos Bresser Pereira and then under Mailson de Nóbrega, a civil servant who had worked under the military governments, who came to office in January 1988, after Bresser Pereira had resigned in protest over Sarney's refusal to allow capital gains taxation as part of his economic stabilisation programme. Brazil lifted the moratorium, began talks with the IMF and eventually, in February 1988, started negotiations with the creditor banks over a further rescheduling. The Prodigal Son had returned home.

By then, too, the Peruvian initiative was floundering. In 1985 and 1986, the plan had worked well. Inflation came down, domestic demand picked up and the government was able to keep the exchange rate under control. Though the government failed to keep debt payments down to the promised 10 per cent of exchange earnings, there was an appreciable easing of the debt burden. In 1986, the economy grew by a remarkable 8.9 per cent, the highest rate in Latin America. García's popularity continued to run at a very high level.

But difficulties had clearly emerged. Because of booming domestic demand, imports soared, eating into the trade surplus. By mid-1986, Peru began to run a trade deficit and the country's foreign reserves began to fall. At the same time, investment ran at a very low level, with the Peruvian business sector failing to respond to the generous incentives the government provided. In July 1987, García unexpectedly decided to nationalise the private banks, in an attempt to steer investment into the priority areas and to stem capital flight. But, unlike the ceiling on debt payments, the nationalisation did not capture the imagination of the Peruvian masses. Instead, it aroused the fierce hatred of the right, which began to campaign fiercely against the government.

The difficulties García faced show clearly that popular mobilisation alone is not enough to create a successful debt strategy. Peru needed an ambitious programme of structural change that would have provided the country with an alternative economic basis, without the old close links with foreign capital.[23] It needed to build up a self-sufficient industrial base, with little reliance on imported goods. It should have developed new export products. It needed to expand the domestic market, tackling the old problems of widespread poverty and severe social inequalities. But none of this was done, and in 1987 the debt strategy began to run out of steam.

The capital haemorrhage continues

By 1988, Latin America's need for relief was as pressing as ever. Surprising as it may seem, the moves by the banks in 1987 had not reduced by one cent the burden imposed on the region. As Citicorp was careful to make clear at the very beginning of the new phase, the added provisions for loss did not mean that the bank was prepared to forgive any Latin American debt. The increase in provisions was merely a defensive move by which the bank had increased its capacity to withstand default, should a recalcitrant debtor one day opt for this action. Citicorp and all the other leading creditor banks still expected the debtor nations to service their debts fully and would do all they could to ensure that they did so. But the main criticism made of Citicorp's initiative by British bankers was precisely that it could be interpreted by the debtor nations as an invitation to default. To loud applause, Robin Leigh-Pemberton, the governor of the Bank of England, warned bankers at a banquet in the City of London in February 1988 against making 'excessive provisions' for fear of sending the 'wrong signals' to debtor countries.[24]

In keeping with the new climate, Latin American nations had become aware that their best course for obtaining some debt relief was through schemes that entailed limited losses for the banks, not ones that look for large sums of new money. The Brazilian finance ministry, under Bresser Pereira, was the first to attempt to take such a course. In July 1987, he sent the banks a proposal by which half of the Brazilian debt due to be rescheduled would be handled in a conventional way, while the other half would be converted, at a heavy discount, into long-term bonds, for which the government would supply special guarantees. Because of the proposed discount, this scheme would for the first time ever entail real losses for the banks. And, somewhat predictably, they reacted indignantly, rejecting the proposal wholesale. With President Sarney unwilling as ever to confront the bankers, the project was dropped, and Brazil moved on to other proposals, eventually accepting talks on a fully conventional rescheduling. If Brazil had hoped that the banks would accept the debt−bond scheme without demur, it made two mistakes: it tried to make it obligatory for all banks involved in the rescheduling; and it did not provide convincing guarantees that the new bonds would be serviced any more regularly than the old debt.

At the end of the year, Mexico came up with the two missing elements and, true to its role as pioneer in the debt crisis, became the first Latin American nation to make a breakthrough on this front. It presented a new swap scheme in which it offered to exchange old Mexican debt for new bonds, payable over 20 years, at a good rate of interest. The Mexican government said that it would guarantee payment of interest on the bonds by offering as collateral US Treasury bonds, which it had bought from the US government in a normal market transaction. The Mexican government thus offered a new and guaranteed financial asset, and one that could be freely traded on the market, complying with the market trend away from debt into securities. But, in return, it asked the banks to accept a heavy discount. Ten dollars of debt would be exchanged, not for ten dollars of bond, but for four or five, depending upon which banking group presented the Mexican government with the most attractive proposal.

If fully subscribed, the scheme would have reduced Mexican debt by about $20 billion, one-fifth of the total. The debt-servicing burden would not have been reduced by as much, because a fairly high rate of interest would have been payable on the new bonds, but the savings would have been appreciable. The scheme had attractive features for the banks: rock-solid guarantee for interest payment (US treasury bonds); voluntary nature; reliance on market mechanisms. Even so, most banks were reluctant to take part, probably through fear of establishing a precedent in which the creditors bore real, if limited, losses. In the end, Mexico issued bonds worth only $2.5 billion, just a quarter of the planned value. It seemed that tough action by the debtors was required even to convince the creditors to accept very small bosses.

Notes

1. See Latin America Bureau, *The Dance of the Millions*, London, 1988.
2. Bernardo Kucinski, 'Where parallel loans may meet', *Euromoney*, January 1984.
3. *Financial Times*, 20 August 1982.
4. *Financial Times*, 18 August 1982.
5. Latin America Bureau, *The Poverty Brokers — The IMF and Latin America*,

London, 1983.
6. Robert Devlin, 'Renegotiation of Latin America's debt, *Cepal Review* no. 20.
7. *Financial Times*, 15 November 1982.
8. *Euromoney*, October 1982.
9. In an interview with Bernardo Kucinski.
10. Ricardo Ffrench-Davis, in an interview with Sue Branford.
11. Reginald Herbold Green, 'Third World sovereign debt renegotiation, 1980–86 and after: procedures, paradigms and portents', discussion paper, Institute of Development Studies, University of Sussex, December 1986.
12. *Financial Times*, 10 February 1983.
13. Anatole Kaletsky, *The Costs of Default*, A Twentieth Century Fund Paper, Priority Press Publications, New York, 1985.
14. Jorge Schwarzer, 'La experiencia Argentina de renegociación de su deuda externa: limitaciones y perspectivas', mimeographed paper presented at conference on Latin American debt at Campinas University, Brazil, December 1985.
15. Harold Lever and Christopher Huhne, *Debt and Danger: The World Financial Crisis*, Penguin Special, 1985.
16. Jorge Schwarzer, op.cit.
17. *Clarín*, a leading Argentine newspaper, 1 April 1984.
18. Jorge Schwarzer, op.cit.
19. See John Crabtree's chapter on Peru in Latin America Bureau, *The Dance of the Millions*, London, 1988.
20. *Financial Times*, 1 December 1985.
21. IBCA Banking Analysis Ltd newsletter, August 1987.
22. Ibid.
23. See John Crabtree, op.cit.
24. *Financial Times*, 2 February 1988.

The commercial banks profit at Latin America's expense

(For many ordinary people, one of the most distasteful aspects of the Latin American debt crisis has been the way in which the big commercial banks have continued to make huge profits, on paper at least, from the debt crisis, though it has thrown millions of Latin Americans out of work and led to a significant increase in malnutrition, particularly among children. How has this happened?

During the 1970s, the world's big banks, particularly the nine money-centre banks in the US and the four high-street banks in the UK, lent so heavily to Latin America that these loans became larger than these banks' net assets, that is, the assets that they really own, not the money that they borrow from clients and misleadingly call their 'assets'. For it is only these net assets — also known as the shareholders' equity — that could be used to bail out the bank in the event of a banking crisis.

In March 1984, the nine money-centre banks in the US had loans worth $49 billion to the five leading Latin American debtors (Brazil, Mexico, Argentina, Venezuela and Chile). This was equivalent to 165.1 per cent of the shareholders' equity (*see* Table 10.1). The situation of the four UK banks was similar. At the end of 1984, they had outstanding loans to these same five countries worth £14.1 billion, equivalent to 156.6 per cent of the shareholders' equity (*see* Table 10.2). All these ratios are very high and they mean that, in the event of two or three of these countries ceasing payment so that their debts are considered losses, the bank would go bankrupt. Midland was more exposed than any other bank, with its loans to these five countries accounting for a remarkable 314.5 per cent of its shareholders' equity.

In the run-up to the debt crisis, the banks profited greatly from this wide exposure, with their Latin American lending bringing in very high profits at apparently little risk, with bankers, like John Reed from Citicorp, reassuring shareholders that 'countries don't go bankrupt'. Let us work out the kind of return that a heavily exposed bank, like Midland, was making. From 1980 to 1982 spreads varied from 2.0 per cent to 2.4 per cent for Latin American borrowers. With total loans to Latin America of £5.3 billion, Midland must have earned about £117 million from the spread (2.2 per cent of £5.3 billion). As Midland's loans to Latin America represented 14.1 per cent of its total lending, and were therefore underpinned by a similar proportion of its shareholders' equity, that is, £238 million (14.1 per cent of £1.7 billion), Midland must have had an excellent return on its capital, of about 49.0 per cent.

But with the onset of the debt crisis, profits grew rather than diminished for the banks. For when the spectre of widespread Latin American default became real, the banks had little option in the short term but to carry on lending, albeit at a reduced rate, for fear of seeing their worst nightmares come true. But by then the banks, seriously concerned that lending to Latin America was a very real risk, felt justified in increasing their charges. So, as well as continuing to charge high spreads (or even raising them), the banks demanded additional commissions, of 1–1.5 per cent, on the value of the debt rescheduled. If we assume that half of Midland's loans were rescheduled during the first round of reschedulings, then it had additional earnings of at least £17 million, pushing up its overall return to a remarkable 56 per cent.

But by now the precarious nature of these high profits was clear. Such a high return was only possible because the banks were lending Latin America part of the money. It was clear that the whole castle of cards could come tumbling, if the flow was interrupted. Far from being proud of the profits they were making, banks became ashamed of their heavy exposure.

At times, the banks went to extraordinary lengths to play down their Latin American exposure. In his address in Barclays Bank's 1984 report and accounts, Sir Timothy Bevan, chairman of the group, stated: 'Whilst, of course, we cannot know other banks' exposure with certainty, an analyst's

Table 10.2
The weight of Latin American debt in the four leading British banks
(value of outstanding loans in £ million, end 1984)

	Brazil	Mexico	Argentina	Venezuela	Total for Latin America	Latin American lending as % of shareholders' equity
Barclays	571	1,010	450	278	3,015	115.9
Lloyds	1,857	1,181	556	554	5,281	257.4
Midland	1,871	1,590	757	400	5,300	314.5
National Westminster	795	700	475	250	2,712	102.4

Sources: Banks' annual reports and accounts, 1984.

report, based on 1983 figures, which is accurate as far as we are concerned, shows that our exposure to South America, the chief source of misgivings, is the least, usually clearly the least, of the major US and British banks'.

The statement was clearly intended to reassure the bank's shareholders, who were known to be worried by Barclays' heavy exposure to South Africa, of £5.8 billion, equivalent to over twice the shareholders' equity of £2.6 billion and far higher than any other major British bank. It was comforting for them to know that, even if Barclays was vulnerable in South Africa, it was little exposed in South America, the developing region which was widely regarded as the most serious risk.

All very fine, except for one problem. Although Sir Timothy did not say so, the report to which he was referring seems to have been the one published by De Zoete & Bevan, the London stockbrokers (of which, Sir Timothy announced in the same address, Barclays was purchasing a controlling interest). This report, in which Barclays was duly found to be the least exposed of the major US and British banks, looked at loans to 'South America', that is, Latin America excluding Central America and, far more significantly, Mexico. This detail must have been overlooked by the majority of shareholders for whom, as for the vast majority of British people, the terms 'South America' and 'Latin America' mean very much the same thing.

No reason was given for excluding Mexico. It may not be a complete coincidence that, according to the 1984 figures, Barclays had lent £1 billion to Mexico, twice as much as to any other Latin American nation. Without Mexico, loans to South America stood at 77 per cent of the shareholders' equity. With Mexico, loans to Latin America rose to 116 per cent, ranking Barclays above National Westminster and several of the US money-centre banks in the list of most heavily exposed banks. Loans to Latin America and South Africa, taken together, accounted for £8.8 billion, equivalent to 340 per cent of the shareholders' equity. It was scarcely surprising that Sir Timothy wanted to find some kind of reassurance for his shareholders.

11. Conclusion: In Favour of Default

Where the authors argue that the only moral obligation of Latin American governments is to end the capital haemorrhage

> Now here, you see, it takes all the running you can do, to stay in the same place. If you want to get somewhere else, you must run at least twice as fast as that.
>
> **Lewis Carroll**, *Through the Looking Glass*

One clear message emerges from the long and tortuous story of the Latin American debt crisis — the present bleeding of resources out of the continent is imperialist exploitation on an unprecedented scale. As we saw in Chapter 8, Latin America borrowed the enormous sum of $272.9 billion between the end of 1976 and the end of 1981. But almost all (91.6 per cent) of this money went straight back to the banks: in debt-servicing (62.2 per cent); in other outflows, particularly capital flight (20.5 per cent); and in the building up of international reserves (8.9 per cent). Only a tiny proportion — 8.4 per cent ($22.9 billion) — was brought into the continent, possibly (but not always) to be used in development projects.

In our opinion, the money that did not enter the continent cannot be considered the responsibility of ordinary Latin American people. It is 'illegitimate' debt, either because it was caused by the surge in US interest rates, a factor completely outside Latin America's control, or because it was illicit profiteering by the Latin American ruling elites, with the connivance not of the Latin American people, most of whom were completely unaware of what was happening, but of the commercial banks. We believe that ordinary Latin Americans should feel morally responsible only for the amount that came into the continent.

As we saw in the first chapter, Latin America sent to the banks in the industrialised countries, in net terms, $159.1 billion between the end of 1981 and the end of 1986. These remittances were enough to pay back the 'legitimate' debt several times over, even if you accept that Latin America should pay a reasonably high rate of interest. But, in the Alice in Wonderland world of international finance, this net transfer was not enough even to pay the interest, so yet more money had to be borrowed. The gross foreign debt grew by a further enormous amount — $115.2 billion. Despite the very large payments, Latin America's debt burden is growing heavier and heavier. Far from overcoming the crisis, almost all the big debtor nations are still having to be periodically bailed out by so-called 'rescue packages', drawn up by the US government and the commercial banks. The political cost of these packages, in terms of outside interference in domestic policy-making, is considerable.

It is evident that the foreign debt has become a mechanism which the industrialised countries are using, not only to extract a permanent income, but to exert political domination. Latin America's relationship with its creditors is no longer that of a normal market transaction, but has become one of extreme exploitation, similar to that between a conqueror and a nation defeated in war. It is not for nothing that both Fidel Castro and the Brazilian labour leader, Luis Inacio da Silva ('Lula'), have referred to the debt crisis as 'the Third World War'.

The exploitative nature of the relationship becomes evident if we draw a parallel with a normal business contract in the industrialised world, such as the taking out of a mortgage by a couple in Britain so that they can purchase a house. In this case, a certain sum of money is borrowed by the couple, at a floating interest rate, to be repaid to the building society over a long period, usually 20 or 25 years, under mutually acceptable conditions. Imagine the outrage felt by this couple and, indeed, by all house-buyers with a mortgage, if a British government, of whatever party affiliation, were to adopt monetary policies that led to a fourfold increase in the mortgage rate, so that the couple's monthly payments increased from, let us say, £150 to £600. Many families would run heavily into debt, and it would be highly likely that the government that took this very unpopular measure would be voted out of office at the next election. In this way, mortgage-holders, as a group, have considerable power that can be used against any party that attempts to damage their collective interests. The contract works because all parties concerned — the mortgage-holders, the government and the building societies — have sanctions that they can impose. Though not equal, the distribution of power between the parties is not violently lopsided.

Latin America's 'big stick'

The *poor* in Latin America (and indeed, to a lesser extent, the poor in Britain) do not have a weapon at their disposal that gives them similar direct leverage, though they are the ones who foot the bill. But, it could be argued, the very size of Latin America's debt gives the *governments* of the region real bargaining power. When interest rates on Latin America's debt rose fourfold, with Libor, rising in real terms (that is, with world inflation discounted) from 1–2 per cent in 1978 to 6 per cent in 1981, why did Latin American governments not threaten to repudiate the debt, at least as a means to extract concessions? Why did they meekly accept full responsibility and impose such a harsh 'adjustment' that the region's long-term future has been compromised?

The commonest answer to this question is simply that the power relationship is unequal. For all the havoc that a Latin American default could cause in the world banking system, the country that defaulted would itself be hurt the most. The industrialised nations, particularly the US, it is said, have such a range of economic and political reprisals at their disposal that they could bring to its knees any Latin American nation that might seriously challenge their authority. But is this the case?

Anatole Kaletsky puts forward a very different view in an interesting book entitled *The Costs of Default*[1] (it is said that his first choice for a title was 'The Benefits of Default', but that this was considered by the publisher to be too provocative). He looks at the possible reprisals that could be inflicted by the private banks on a debtor nation in default. He states:

Many participants in international banking appear to believe that creditors could bring a defaulting country's trade almost to a standstill by attaching a defaulter's ships, airplanes and export cargoes whenever they ventured into the jurisdiction of a nation prepared to recognise the judgement or a US or English court (depending on which law governs the loan agreement in default). Such a belief . . . is unrealistic. Individual citizens of a country — including corporate citizens — are in no way liable for the debts of their governments. The courts will never punish a private Argentine wheat exporter or a private Brazilian airline, for example, for the defaults of their states.

After looking at all the possible measures available to the private banks, Kaletsky concludes:

Bankers' hopes — and borrowers' fears — that crippling costs could be imposed on recalcitrant debtor nations through court action appear to be greatly exaggerated . . . Taking all these direct and indirect costs and benefits together, legal action would not appear to be a very serious menace for a major borrower considering default; debtors as big as Brazil, Mexico, Argentina or Venezuela might rationally consider such a threat to be like a bluff in a poker game.

However, the situation changes dramatically if the creditor government decides also to impose sanctions:

The arsenal of potential sanctions available to the United States, Britain and other creditor nations is almost unlimited . . . The political branches of creditor country governments have almost limitless powers to deploy against defaulting debtors, if they so desire. Such government reprisals cannot even be circumscribed by current laws or precedents, since it is always in the power of Parliament or Congress to change the laws (including those governing sovereign immunity) if they see fit.

But Kaletsky then argues persuasively that the creditor government is highly unlikely to take the extreme option of imposing the whole range of sanctions. Much would depend on the form the default took. A skilful debtor nation, Kaletsky suggests, would declare what he calls a 'conciliatory default', that is, a default on medium-term bank debts (which make up the major part of Latin America's debt), presented regretfully as a painful necessity, not as a political challenge to the world's financial system. In such circumstances, 'the interest of foreign traders, multinational direct investors and providers of trade finance would be left unscathed'. In other words, a powerful lobby in favour of a negotiated settlement would be created in the creditor country. As Kaletsky puts it:

Publicly the multinationals could be expected to maintain a tactful silence in the event of a default. Privately, they would lobby hard in favour of a speedy negotiated solution that preserved the security of industrial investment in the defaulting country, whatever it meant for bank profits.

Moreover, the creditor governments, he argues, are well aware of the highly disruptive impact of a large Latin American default on the commercial banks and the economy as a whole. 'Recent simulations have suggested that a default by the whole of Latin America would cost the United States nearly 2.5 per cent of gross national product in lost output and 1.1 million jobs within one year.' It would be a powerful incentive to the US government to avoid outright confrontation. Kaletsky concludes:

> A close look at the cards suggests a deck which is stacked in favour of the borrowers, not the bankers. The legal and financial deterrents to default are minimal in comparison to the potential financial gains which some debtor nations might make by reducing or evading their obligations.

Moreover, the cost of default, he says, would be a one-off blow, in many ways easier to deal with than today's steady draining of resources. Its impact would lessen quite rapidly and credibility would be regained. 'In this connection, it is worth remembering that nearly every one of today's major debtors had already defaulted massively on sovereign debts in the 1930s.'

Since Kaletsky published his book in 1985, the case for 'conciliatory default' has strengthened considerably. As we saw in Chapter 10, all the leading commercial banks have increased dramatically their provisions for Third World losses, in the wake of the Brazilian moratorium. Though a simultaneous default by all major Latin American debtors could still spark off a chain of bankruptcies, the world's banking system is in a much stronger position than in 1982. On the one hand, this weakens Latin America's position, for it means that the banks can withstand for much longer a protracted confrontation. But, on the other hand, it strengthens the case for 'responsible' default. The banks can now quite clearly afford to take some losses on their Latin American lending. The bankers' much-repeated insistence that they expect all Latin American loans to be scrupulously serviced, despite the swollen provisions, sounds increasingly hollow.

Most of the arguments presented by Kaletsky are now commonly known. The key questions become: why have the governments of the big Latin American debtors been so reluctant to build up a debt strategy based on default? Any why have the governments of the smaller nations been so slow to create an effective debtors' cartel that would give them the collective leverage to default?

Why Latin American governments fail to use their power

The common answer to this query is very simple: corruption. Latin American government officials, it is argued, are bought off by the industrialised countries. As they are accumulating massive personal wealth from the status quo, government officials are disinclined to rebel, except for a few mavericks, who soon fall from power. It is, indeed, virtually impossible to imagine Martínez de Hoz of Argentina or Delfim Netto of Brazil at the head of a debtors' cartel.

But this explanation, based on the experience of individuals, seems to us to lack sociological basis. Only a relatively small fraction of Latin America's ruling elites has access to these gravy-trains. To service its debt, Latin America has mutilated its economy, failing to carry out investment in productive capacity, new technology and basic infrastructure essential to the region's future development. As we saw in Chapter 1, Latin America has been going through a process of 'de-development' that threatens to leave the continent in a permanent state of underdevelopment and dependency. It seems clear that such destructive policies are damaging the interests not only of ordinary Latin American people, who are losing their jobs and going hungry, but also of the ruling elites, who run the risk of losing the economic basis of their domination. If Latin America's long-term future is being compromised by the failure of the governments to stand up to the foreign creditors, why haven't the ruling elites simply replaced the corrupt officials with more honest and more courageous representatives?

There seem to be two interlinked factors. First of all, the current policies favour a much larger group within the ruling elites than those benefiting directly from pay-offs. In particular, as was shown in Chapter 5, the pressing need under the existing scheme for Latin American nations to maximise dollar earnings at the expense of domestic development, leads to the adoption of incentives that benefit all businessmen (and, to a growing extent, businesswomen) who earn dollars, be they exporters from manufacturing, farming or mining sectors, or tourist operators. These people are likely to put their own short-term interests before their country's long-term development needs. As many writers have pointed out, a large part of Latin America's bourgeoisie is not nationalistic in its views, but content to be integrated with the industrialised economies in a subordinate way.

Secondly, there are sound political reasons for caution among the ruling elites, even among that faction that is seriously alarmed by Latin America's current decline and would like to see the process reversed. As the Peruvian experience has shown, any government that wished to challenge the rules of the game established by the creditors would not only have to mobilise massive popular support around the new radical policy, but also be prepared to implement new domestic policies to tide the country over a difficult period of foreign currency shortage.

This is because the creditors would back down and make concessions only if they believed that the government was serious in its intention and prepared for confrontation if negotiations failed. It was precisely because the creditors realised that the Brazilian government was not prepared either to withstand a long period of confrontation with its creditors or to carry out the necessary social and economic reforms at home that they refused to make real concessions in the wake of the Brazilian moratorium in February 1987.

But such policies are dangerous for the ruling elites. The masses, once aroused, are unwilling to limit their demands to the reforms prescribed by the government. They will tend to broaden out their programme to include demands for far-reaching changes in domestic policies, such as greater political freedoms, radical measures to reduce inequalities in income distribution and effective agrarian reform. In many Latin American countries, particularly Mexico and Brazil, the ruling elites seem well aware of the dangers they would face in the wake of wide-scale popular mobilisation. Indeed, almost all factions of Latin America's bourgeoisie appear to prefer to see their countries slip back into underdevelopment and dependency rather than run the risk of being forced into radical social and economic reforms.

Pushing for change from the grassroots

If the ruling elites have been reluctant to stand up to the creditors, why haven't the ordinary people of Latin America forced them to change their policies? The answer to this question seems to be linked to Latin America's political history. As we showed in Chapter 5, Latin America has a long history of revolutionary struggle, in which thousands have died in the attempt to change society. But, as is happening now with particular intensity in Central America, these revolutionary movements have been violently repressed, with massive US assistance. Only occasionally, as in Cuba and Nicaragua, have the revolutionaries won through.

As a result, Latin America has not developed a tradition of non-revolutionary reform, in which, as happened in Europe in the 19th century, the state has acted as a mediator between capital and labour and has forced the bourgeoisie to accept reforms, as times quite radical reforms, which defuse popular discontent and increase the bourgeoisie's long-term chances of survival. This is largely because the state in Latin America's development has had a different role, investing heavily in productive capacity and in infrastructure. Rather than helping to redress social injustice, the state in Latin America has been a powerful agent of capital accumulation and one of the primary forces creating social inequalities.[2] The long years of military rule in the 1970s and early 1980s in most of South America reinforced this tendency, putting an end to the limited reforms that were being carried out. Only in a few isolated cases, such as the Peruvian initiative under Alan García, has the bourgeoisie responded positively to popular pressure by adopting a radical debt policy.

It is against this background that progressive groups in Latin America must formulate their foreign debt policy. At an ethical level, we have no doubts as to what this policy should be. Far from having a moral obligation to the creditors to go on paying the debt, the governments of Latin America have a moral obligation to their people to stop paying the debt. However, we do not mean by this that the first step a progressive government should take, were it to come to power in any Latin American nation, should be debt repudiation or debt default. It is obvious that governments must be pragmatic. While for one of the big debtors the advantages to be gained from a halt in debt-servicing, particularly if it were presented in a fairly conciliatory fashion, as Kaletsky suggests, would almost certainly be far greater than the possible reprisals from the moratorium, this might not be the case for one of the smaller and more vulnerable Latin American nations, such as El Salvador or Uruguay. For them, the reprisals from debt repudiation could bring greater suffering to the people than the present heavy debt burden. These countries urgently need to learn to co-ordinate their debt strategies, possibly with the collaboration of one of the bigger debtor nations. The underlying objective behind the strategy must be to reduce the capital haemorrhage, however that can best be achieved.

Until recently, there were remarkably few contacts between the debtor nations in different parts of the developing world. But slowly this is beginning to change. Latin American groups are beginning to talk to groups in African countries that, despite their greater dependence on official (rather than commercial) debt, are also experiencing capital outflows that are having a ruinous impact on the local economy. Just as in Latin America, many groups in these countries are also carrying out vigorous internal debates as to the best foreign debt strategy. Links with progressive groups in the industrialised countries are also growing quickly, under the aegis of the non-governmental agencies and the churches, both Catholic and Protestant. But as yet there have been no effective international campaigns, organised simultaneously in the industrialised countries and the developing world.

There is little likelihood that any of the major Latin American debtors will adopt a truly radical debt policy in the immediate future. It is much more likely that the region will continue to obtain small, piecemeal concessions from the creditors, which will have to be assessed with considerable caution to see if they represent a real advance or merely an adaptation on the part of the creditors to the changing face of the debt crisis.

Since 1985, the Latin American governments have proved less efficient at producing huge trade surpluses, partly because their exports have been hurt by falling commodity prices (particularly oil) and partly because of the enormous difficulty in keeping imports at rock bottom year after year. As a result, the trade surplus fell from $34.3 billion in 1985 to $18.0 billion in 1986 (*see* Table 2.2, p. 17) and an estimated $22.7 billion in 1987. As these resources have been insufficient, debt servicing problems have been increasing. Every two or three months, one of the big debtors and several of the smaller ones have fallen into arrears and have had to be saved from default by yet another rescue package. The commercial banks, under pressure from the IMF, have had to cover the shortfall to prevent default. As a result, bank lending (official and private) rose from $23.6 billion in 1985 to $31.5 billion in 1986, and the net transfer of resources out of the region fell somewhat, from $34 billion in 1985 to $26 billion in 1986.

The banks clearly want to stop providing this new money, but at the same time they cannot accept widespread default. As they cannot indefinitely have their cake and eat it too, some solution will have to be found. For them, the only way out of the dilemma seems to be to reduce the value of the debt service payments so that they are more in line with the region's real capacity to pay, without outside funding. The banks seem extremely reluctant to accept any new deal that entails real losses for them, probably because they are afraid of a stampede by Latin American debtors once a crack has opened in their defences. But new deals, perhaps tougher versions of the Mexican debt−bond swap, that entail modest but real reductions in the debt burden, seem likely. If the banks do not agree to them voluntarily, one of the bigger debtor nations will eventually impose such a scheme unilaterally. With the banks' increased provisions, the case for passing on part of the benefit to Latin America has become overwhelming.

Whatever form it takes, the debt relief will be presented as a real breakthrough in the debt crisis and a victory for Latin America. But the new scheme will have to be assessed with caution. If it results in a gentler flow of resources out of the region — the 'net transfer' in our tables — then it will represent a real advance. But if, as seems likely, it merely enables the banks to lend less without forcing the region into default, but does nothing, or next to nothing, to stem the outflow, then it will have brought no benefits to the people of the region.

Though the pace is very slow, Latin American governments are hardening their foreign debt policies, under pressure from mass-based organisations, and this tendency is likely to continue. There is already a remarkable understanding among ordinary Latin American people of the basic causes of their poverty and falling living standards. One has only to hear the number of times 'the IMF' and 'US imperialism' are mentioned in protests over food shortages or increases in bus fares to appreciate this.

Slowly, very slowly, popular pressure in Latin America for an end to debt exploitation is building up. Indeed, the one positive aspect of the debt crisis has been the way in which it has made a growing sector of the population aware of the pressing need for far-reaching social change. But, while an effective political force is painfully constructed, the bleeding of resources out of the continent continues.

Notes

1. Anatole Kaletsky, *The Costs of Default*, A Twentieth Century Fund Paper, Priority Press Publications, New York, 1985.
2. Sylvia Ann Hewlett and Richard S. Weinert, *Brazil and Mexico — Patterns in Late Development*, Institute for the Study of Human Issues, Philadelphia, 1982.

Index